The WEALTH COACH

The WEALTH COACH

Bradley J. Sugars

Publisher
CITIES

Publisher: Jesse Krieger

Write to Jesse@JesseKrieger.com if you are interested in publishing through Lifestyle Entrepreneurs Press.

Publications or foreign rights acquisitions of our catalogue books.
Learn More: www.LifestyleEntrepreneursPress.com

ISBN: 9781946697844

CONTENTS

Introduction

Coaching and educating people on how wealth happens is not an easy task. Then again, few worthwhile endeavors ever are. Transferring my—or in this case—"The Wealth Coach's" knowledge and expertise to others is definitely a two-way street. Let's assume you wanted to make a complex dish for which only I had the recipe. Giving you the recipe would be simple. However, it would be up to you to shop for the ingredients, understand the directions (and if needed, seek clarification), and be able to follow those directions. Most importantly, you would have to *want* to make the dish and get cooking!

Fortunately, my recipe is simple and presented here in an easy-to-follow, entertaining story of a family who must start their wealth-building from scratch at different times in their lives due to a financially devastating crisis. When The Wealth Coach sits down with his students, he is essentially giving them a simple step-by-step recipe for creating wealth.

I wrote this book as a story so that you could see the blending of regular, everyday life while going through the process of patiently creating wealth. There are many roads to wealth, but as you will find in the following chapters, some very tried and true principles work when you apply them—principles that are guaranteed to work whether you start as a kid or an adult in your mid-sixties. These principles are your road to wealth.

By following the stories of Mitch, Amy, and their mother Kim on very different journeys to wealth, you will see just how these principles work. More importantly, you will learn how you can put them to work for you.

Creating wealth for yourself involves neither magic nor luck. There are no "get-rich-quick" schemes, but it doesn't have to be drudgery either. It *is* about strategy, planning, and persevering combined with patience and self-discipline. I am going to teach you how to apply these principles, and then it's all up to you.

Be rich or be broke. It is truly your choice.

Chapter 1

Surprise!

Amy and Mitch McConnell, twins of a California beauty and a father they never knew, sat eagerly at a plush velvet booth at Lorraine's, the finest steakhouse in town. It was their sixteenth birthday. Kim, their mother, had wanted to give them some sort of "sweet sixteen" party at their swanky Malibu beach home, but Mitch wanted nothing to do with it—*that was for girls*. Instead, the family hosted a small dinner party where Kim and her husband, Bryce Peters, decided to unveil the gift of a lifetime.

The twins waited patiently for their mother and Bryce to finish hobnobbing at the bar and come give them their big birthday surprise.

Bryce and Kim had only been married for four years. He made quite a decent living as an IT consultant, but nearly all his earnings went to his one passion: Kim. Not a particularly handsome man but an expert in his field and a decade Kim's senior, he met Kim five years prior and knew he *had* to have her.

Kim, who hadn't remarried since the twins' father disappeared without a trace when they were just two years old, had assumed early on that her modeling career would be sufficient to support herself and the twins for quite some time. As long as she took good care of herself—her perfect figure and flawless skin, silky blonde hair, and wet blue eyes—she estimated that she had a good twenty years in the business. And if that wasn't the case, it was just like her mama always told her: "it is just as easy to marry a rich man as a poor one."

Though Bryce wasn't her ultimate dream guy, he swept her off her feet with gifts, flowers, dinners, trips, and overwhelming admiration. One time when her car broke down, he had a brand new Cobra Mustang—in his name—delivered directly to her modeling shoot as a gift. Besides the extravagant gifts, he made her laugh, was kind to the twins, and she never had to think about money. In fact, Bryce insisted that Kim give up the modeling. He didn't want his wife to work—especially modeling lingerie and other skimpy outfits. He wanted her to accompany him on business trips to give him the prestige that only a beautiful, poised woman like her can bring to an older man with ho-hum looks and an arrogant personality.

Thus, she settled.

Neither she nor the twins ever worried about money once Bryce came along. Before Bryce, Kim was able to give the twins a decent lifestyle, and they never wanted for much. Unfortunately, she lived paycheck-to-paycheck, never thinking of the future.

Bryce took charge of all the bills, taxes, insurance, and bank accounts. He furnished Kim with a joint checking account that always contained a few thousand dollars, and a credit card with a $10,000 limit he allowed her to use at her discretion.

In reality, her only job was to be Bryce's stunning trophy wife and adoring mother to the twins, whom she truly cherished and took pride in rearing mainly on her own.

Around 6 o'clock, a driver had picked up the twins from the beach home, and the maître d' escorted them to a large round booth with 32 white and red roses as the centerpiece: there were sixteen apiece; white symbolized innocence, red, love, and together, unity—a very creative choice, Kim thought, given that Mitch and Amy were united as twins. When the twins entered the room, the pianist immediately switched from his current piece and played "*Happy Birthday*" as the other patrons sang along and clapped.

Obviously well-known about town, Kim and Bryce felt obliged to mingle just a bit after the twins arrived. "Just sit down babies, and we'll be right over," Kim whispered as she held them tightly. "Have we got a surprise for you!"

Fifteen minutes later, Kim shot the twins a look of impatience after having to chit-chat with Bryce's business associates while the birthday boy and girl waited patiently for their birthday dinner and big surprise. Kim would have no more of it, and she insisted that she and Bryce excuse themselves from the bar to join Mitch and Amy.

Their waiting for the surprise continued throughout five courses, as Bryce and Kim grinned from ear-to-ear: Kim because the twins were happy, and Bryce because Kim was. Finally Bryce, with a huge smile, handed Kim a thick manila envelope with big satin pink and blue bows. It was addressed "Amy and Mitch—Happy 16th!" Kim smiled knowingly and passed it to the twins, as they excitedly yet gingerly tore it open together.

The package was from renowned travel agency Segal Travel, and it contained four first-class tickets to Maui and an itinerary of their week-long stay in an exquisite two-bedroom suite at the Grand Wailea, plus brochures of the resort and other activities they could choose from while there. Also enclosed were two $1,000 Visa gift cards and several store gift cards of various denominations.

The trip was scheduled for three months from that date: June 16. The kids would be out of school by then. It would give Kim time to par up her resort wardrobe, and Bryce would have a chance to finish the project he had been contracted to complete at the rate of $300 per hour, which, unbeknownst to Kim, was the sole income financing this extravagant gift.

Bryce knew he was completely mismanaging their finances, but seeing her and the kids so happy meant the world to him. He kept telling himself that he would get it together and start putting the money he made to better use. He wanted to ensure a future for his new family.

After cake, champagne, gifts from other well-wishers who knew the family, and a few dances to songs like "*Sixteen Candles*" and "*She Was Only Sixteen*," the four headed home in their brand new burgundy Jaguar XE. The family had traveled together before, but usually Kim and Bryce left the twins home, as they were typically in school.

They pulled up to the drive late at night. Waves were crashing against the stilts the home was built upon, and the moon nothing but a sliver of a crescent. Bryce yawned. "Honey, I'm tired," he said weakly. "I'm going to check my server and head to bed. You and the kids unload the car," and he wandered inside.

"We got it, mom," they said in unison, as twins often do.

"Thanks, babies." She hugged them one more time and stepped back to look at her teen twins, and said "And happy birthday again!"

Mitch popped the trunk to the Jag—which he had secretly wished would have been his gift—and Amy grabbed an armful of bags containing gifts, cards, and leftover cake. Suddenly, a blood-curdling scream came from inside the house. It was their mother. They dropped everything and ran inside.

Kim knelt next to a bluish, unconscious Bryce. "Call 911," she cried, "one of you call 911!" Mitch was already on it. Amy stood still, completely in shock and at least three shades paler than her normal porcelain skin tone as they heard sirens wail. Within seconds, they saw lights that enveloped the entire street in a colorful blaze of red, blue, and yellow, and counted at least ten uniformed paramedics, police officers, and firefighters chaotically traipsing through the house, trying without avail to revive Bryce.

Finally one paramedic, who had tried three times to resuscitate Bryce, shook his head solemnly. He looked at his watch and softly reported, "Time of death, 11:14 p.m."

• • •

Two days had passed. Kim's mother, Angie, had flown in from Sacramento right away to help with the final arrangements. Like the twins, Kim never really knew her father, and Bryce's parents had long since passed in a car accident.

Only 53 years old and quite young for a heart attack, all conditions were right for someone his age to have one: overweight, excessive alcohol use, no exercise, and a mountain of stress.

It seemed like everyone was in a state of functional shock, not really knowing how to feel. Bryce and Kim's marriage had had some problems—Kim knew Bryce was obsessed with her and would do anything to make her happy. She had to admit to herself that at times she had taken advantage of that. To the twins Bryce was *new*, but he was the only father they ever had, and it was sort of nice to be part of a family with a dad in it. Still, it seemed like no one was particularly devastated. Sad, confused, upset—but not devastated. For the first two days Kim paced around the house, straightening this-and-that. She cooked for the kids but didn't eat much herself, and when she could sleep she dreamt of being alone in a barren wasteland, never able to find another living soul. She sat up in her bed, knowing she would have to do *something* soon.

"Kim," her mother, Angie, said softly, resting a comforting hand on her shoulder and awakening her from another bad dream, "you need to make arrangements, honey."

Kim looked down, staring at nothing in particular, yet couldn't bring herself to speak.

"Honey," Angie said a little more firmly, "do you know where Bryce's will is?"

Angie shook her head.

"Okay, did he even have one? Life insurance? Bank accounts?" Angie got more insistent as the twins secretly peeked through the slats from the upstairs hall.

Finally, for the first time since Bryce died, Angie burst into tears. "Mama, I don't know! I don't know anything. He just always took care of *everything*!"

The twins looked at each other in a mix of fear and sadness. Their mother had always seemed so tough and independent. How could she not know of their financial situation?

Angie had the bad feeling that a mother's intuition can sometimes bring. "Come on," she said, grabbing Kim's hand. "It's time for us to go through that office."

Reluctantly, her daughter followed.

The credenza in Bryce's office was locked, and Kim had no idea where to find the key. Angie retrieved a steak knife from the kitchen and proceeded to jimmy the lock open. There were files and file folders, invoices from clients, and check stubs. Also present were four years worth of completed tax returns that Kim had signed, with signed checks attached that Bryce had obviously (willfully?) neglected to mail. Next to this mish-mash of papers lay a thick folder with miscellaneous past-due notices, including the one for the new Jaguar, as well as their Range Rover. Kim had fixed and paid off the loan on her Ford Expedition that she owned prior to meeting Bryce, and it was meant to be for the twins' use once they got their driver's licenses.

"Oh my God," Angie said as she sipped her coffee and leafed through the findings thus far.

"What, mama?" Kim asked.

"Honey, did he have a life insurance policy?"

Kim thought for a second, and then perked up, "Yes. It is for five million dollars, plus mortgage insurance on the home. He told me so when we first moved here."

Angie pulled a piece of paper out of the pile. "Uh huh," Angie said doubtfully, scanning, one eyebrow raised. "And have you seen this policy? Do you know what company it's through?"

Kim thought for a second, and then looked at the paper Angie was skimming. "It's that one!" she said.

Angie read the date and heading: "Regarding Life Insurance Application. Dear Mr. Peters," she read slowly, "thank you for applying for life insurance coverage with Acme. We are sorry to inform you that after careful review and consideration of your medical history, we are unable to provide you coverage. Our decision was based on your records from your cardiologist, Dr. James..."

"Stop, mama!" Kim cried. "Are you saying he lied to me? He *didn't* have life insurance?"

"It looks like it, honey, but let's keep looking," Angie said, weary.

At the end of the day, after going through every paper in Bryce's office, the women's findings culminated in one valid check issued to Bryce. It was from his latest client, for $12,900. There were bank statements in Bryce's name from three different banks showing balances of under $1,000 apiece, and bank statements in both Kim and Bryce's names, the latest of which showed a balance of $2,967.17—the one to which he gave Kim access. There were stacks of unopened bills from the prior month, all past due, including the mortgage.

No will. No cash. No life insurance. One half-drunk bottle of scotch.

The two women, faced with the truth that Kim's ignorance of her financial status in her marginal marriage was *not* bliss, each took a swig out of the scotch. They decided that cremation and a very simple church service would be best, and agreed to discuss Kim's plans for herself and the twins in the morning, after they went to their prestigious private school.

It was obvious, as the women sat down over coffee, that Kim would have to sell the house and hopefully at least break even. She would need to get a job and have the cars voluntarily repossessed, except for the Ford - she owned that outright, and it was in her own name. She would pay a visit to the private school where the twins were attending, as they had just over one year until graduation and both were excelling. Amy's excellence showed mainly academically, while Mitch's claim to high school fame was as a star quarterback for the football team. No matter what, Kim would not take them out of their school.

She took a look at her 4.5 karat Cartier diamond wedding ring, and thought better of chucking it into the ocean. Appraised at $127,000, a jeweler friend told her she would be lucky to get a third of that for it.

With the few assets they truly owned, including the ring, her bank account, the Ford, and the check from Bryce's client, Kim decided to buy a clean, modest home in Oxnard, halfway between the twins' school and Malibu. Thanks to the kind principal, who discounted their tuition, they were able to stay there until graduation.

She figured she had a few months' living expenses while she looked for work. Luckily the Malibu home sold almost immediately, though she neither made nor lost money on it, and little else was in her name.

Like Kim, the twins, who enjoyed the finer things in life yet remained mostly unspoiled, took the dramatic change in lifestyle very well. Kim had done an excellent job of liquidating their lives in just over two months, and now they were basically on the same path they were before Bryce came into the picture.

There was just one thing: the birthday trip to Maui, which was only two weeks away. She had forgotten all about it and hadn't discussed it with the twins since giving it to them the night Bryce died. She didn't even know if they still thought about it. Her first inclination was to cancel, but then she remembered the trip was prepaid and nonrefundable anyway, according to the travel agent. Besides, she really didn't want to take *that* away from the twins too.

She glanced into the mirror. She looked tired. She had stopped doing her hair and makeup every day. Most days, she didn't even shower. In her mind, she looked like a bum.

Amy's grades had slipped a lot in a short time, and she, too, seemed disinterested in her social life or being one of the best-dressed girls at school.

Mitch only got more aggressive and poured his heart into his football practices, but his grades, too, had slipped. The three were tired, depressed, and battle-worn. They had been duped, but they had survived.

Kim had been diligent about hanging onto the several thousand dollars she received by liquidating nearly everything of value. She decided firmly at that moment: *yes, they would take that trip.* They would once again see what it was like to live *as if* they were wealthy, and maybe, just maybe, it would incentivize them to make it a reality this time.

• • •

"Darling," Richard Morgan said as he lovingly stroked his wife's head, "I really think I should cancel the seminar." Richard Morgan, also known as "The Wealth Coach," or even just "Coach" to those who knew him, couldn't rationalize leaving for a week-long seminar on Maui when his wife had just broken her leg in three places while mountain climbing. Though he usually didn't bring her on his tours, this one was special. It was his first on Maui, and he knew how much she loved Hawaii. He actually had planned on mixing business with a little pleasure this time.

"You can't cancel, Coach!" his wife, Lori, pleaded. "I'll be fine. Mom and dad are here, and plus we have Rosa. Besides, the seminar is sold out. Do you know how many people will have a fit if you cancel? You'll probably end up with *two* broken legs!" They both laughed, and she grabbed his arm as the pain was kicking in again.

Rosa, their live-in nanny, housekeeper, cook, and now nurse, cleared her throat to announce her presence. She had been with the couple since the kids were babies, and she had become a cherished member of the family.

"Okay Mrs. Morgan, time for your medication. And *you,* Sir," Rosa said firmly, "are packed and have a flight to catch. Lucy is already in her kennel in the car."

Lucy, another cherished family member, was Coach's prized chocolate lab and second best friend - she always accompanied him on his seminars. She was his reward at the end of the day. She waited patiently behind the black screen of the stage as he gave his classes, waiting for him to run and play with her when the day was over.

Coach kissed his wife and three young children goodbye, thinking how fortunate he was to have such a loving, beautiful partner. She wasn't just a wife, but someone who genuinely contributed to a mutual and fantastic vision. Still, as he climbed into the backseat of the town car, he couldn't help but worry about her. He knew how independent and stubborn she could be. He could only hope she would listen to the doctor and stay in bed unless she, with help, absolutely had to get up.

He tried hard to refocus on both the seminar and the goals he was teaching his clients, who had paid tens of thousands of dollars to learn how to make tens of millions or more.

Lucy, who had a severe disdain for the kennel, looked at him with her murky blue eyes and whimpered slightly.

"Me too, girl," Coach said, opening the kennel door and scratching her head. "Me too."

The driver pulled into Van Nuys Executive Airport a few minutes ahead of schedule. For a summer day in Southern California, the weather seemed more like Midwest tornado season; the sky possessed an ominous shade of grey, complete with muggy air that made the 20-foot trip from the car to the jet nearly intolerable.

Lucy acted strangely, panting and sporadically whining.

"Greetings, Coach!" Jim, the pilot of his Gulfstream 650 said. Motioning him up the stairs, he said, "Sorry I can't say it is a better day for a flight, but once we get up there, it's supposed to be smooth."

The driver loaded Coach's bags and Lucy. The flight attendant, Pamela, offered him a cocktail.

"Just a Perrier please, Pamela," he said, letting Lucy out of her kennel.

The takeoff was rough, and the flight turbulent for most of the trip. Lucy kept pacing, and Coach couldn't seem to get his energy in check, as he usually did.

Chapter 2

The Meeting

The resort was even more opulent than depicted in the brochure. In just a few short years, Bryce had shown the family a lifestyle that they had never dreamt of, but this was better than anywhere the twins had ever been.

"This is unreal!" Mitch exclaimed to Amy as Kim checked in at the front desk. The line was particularly long, as there was some sort of seminar beginning the next day, and it was taking Kim forever to get to the front of the line.

"You're right, Mitch," Amy said, "it *is* unreal. We are only here because mom couldn't get the money back from it!" Then she saw how she had burst her brother's bubble, as he shamefully cowered in agreement. She put her arm around him and said, "But it is truly a tropical paradise. Let's just enjoy it while we are here."

They decided to look around while Kim stood in line. Among parrots, pools, palm trees, tropical drinks, exotic floral arrangements, and ukulele music in the background, there were a few large glossy signs spread throughout the lobby. They all bore the face of a rather handsome gentleman and the words, "The Wealth Coach," followed by the dates, times, and location of the event.

Finally, after a bittersweet tour of their luxury suite, Kim and the twins began to unpack, no one knowing quite how to feel. It felt a little creepy taking advantage of Bryce's dying gift. After all, the trip was for four. He would have been there had he not died.

Kim couldn't take it. She had decided to go ahead with the trip anyways, and decided that come hell or high water, they were all going to have a good time!

Though Kim didn't spend her usual thousands on new clothes for their trip, they had used the gift cards to buy a few new bathing suits and resort outfits. She pulled out an especially stunning Ralph Lauren orchid-patterned dress she had gotten on sale and thought, "Okay, I can still *look* wealthy, at least."

"Kids - pool or dinner?" she asked in an upbeat, yet demanding tone.

Mitch and Amy, mesmerized, had not seen their mother look so glamorous, confident, or *rich* in months—maybe longer. "Come on now!" she smiled, "I can't wait to get down there and get one of their famous pineapple drinks while we watch the sunset."

"Mom?" Mitch asked, "Is it okay if Amy and I have a look around the resort? You go ahead and relax. You deserve it." In reality, Mitch wanted to scope out the girls, and he assumed Amy wanted to see the entire resort. She loved to explore.

"Hmmmm. Okay. Let's see - it is six o'clock now. How about dinner at eight o'clock at The Bistro?" One thing Kim hadn't counted on was that food, drinks, and other incidentals were not prepaid, so she would have to curb these expenses somehow. If Bryce were alive, it would have been The Grand Dining Room or a luau every night. Kim thought about how he would be charging all of it too - on credit he wouldn't have been able to afford. For a second, she felt guilty. Did she pressure him that much into giving her more than he could, or did he simply feel unworthy of being her husband, so he compensated by showering her with material things?

The twins changed into their swimsuits, throwing on appropriate cover-ups to tour the resort, and exploring they went.

• • •

Enduring one of the most turbulent flights he had taken in some time, Coach sighed in relief as the jet landed safely and smoothly four hours later. A car waited to take him and Lucy to the Grand Wailea. The others - Jean, Martin, and Shaw - Coach's marketing and event team, had already been at the resort for a couple days, setting things up and making sure everything was perfect for the following day's seminar.

Check-in went smoothly, but before heading to his villa with Lucy he wanted to assess the meeting facility to make sure that the room and the stage were properly set, and that the energy in the room was just right. His team had never let him down, and the venues were always set up in a way that created an energetic, positive flow. Coach was very particular in that way. He felt that positive energy flow was an important part of a successful event.

The team had absolutely outdone themselves. Not easily impressed, Coach stared in amazement at the grandeur of the event setup. He congratulated the team on an exceptional job, shook their hands, and looked forward to getting settled in his villa. He planned on having a run along the beach with Lucy and ordering room service for dinner.

Coach looked around for Lucy, who usually didn't wander more than a few feet from her owner. He didn't panic, figuring she was just sniffing around. It was a large room.

His personal family cell phone interrupted his attempt to find Lucy.

"Mr. Morgan, I am so sorry to bother you, but Missus is in a lot of pain—"

"Rosa?" Coach was nearly yelling, blocking one ear with his finger to drown out any other noise, "Rosa, is that you?!"

"Si, Mr. Morgan," then nothing but static, then all he could make out was, "Missus...wife...pain."

"Rosa, I will call you right back." he said firmly. "Jean, call this number from a landline!"

Within seconds, Jean had Rosa on the resort's house phone, explaining to Coach that his wife had been trying to be strong so that he wouldn't skip the seminar. But in reality she was in terrible pain, and she hadn't heeded her doctor's advice about staying in bed and always having assistance when getting up to use the restroom. As a result she had fallen, and Rosa wasn't certain if she was in her usual pain or if she actually further damaged herself.

Immediately he phoned Phil Larson, a personal friend, neighbor, client, and physician he had asked to stand by in case anything should happen while he was away.

"Phil, this is Coach. I'm hoping you can go to my house right away."

"Sure, anything Coach. What's up?"

Coach explained the situation, called Rosa back, and talked to his wife. By that time, the good doctor had already given her a shot of Demerol, and she was pain-free for the time being. Luckily she hadn't further injured herself, but Dr. Larson scolded her for getting out of bed unassisted.

He knew Phil would make sure his wife's pain would be under control from here on out, but still, he couldn't help feeling guilty for not being there for her. "Let's see," he thought, "turbulent flight, wife in excruciating pain...and now, where the hell is Lucy?"

He noticed an open door in the back of the room that led to the beach outside, and thought, "oh crap!" As he jogged toward the door, stopping to remove his socks and loafers, he rolled up his pants and thought, "Rich or not, anyone can still have a shit day!"

• • •

As the cotton candy sunset gave way to an infinite indigo sky, Mitch and Amy realized they had forgotten their cell phones in the suite. They had lost all track of time and wondered if they were still even at the resort. All they saw were a bunch of cute, small, but elegant houses and a sign that read "No Swimming. Strong Undertow."

"Mitch!" Amy exclaimed, "What time is it? We are supposed to meet mom by eight o'clock. I don't even know where we are."

Something made Mitch look out past the small houses, which were actually the resort's villas, and past the "No Swimming" sign, where he saw something struggling in the water. A seal, maybe? He ran toward the surf. It wasn't a seal.

"Amy!" he yelled, ripping off his shirt and flip-flops, "It's a dog! It's drowning!" He dove into the rough yet warm water, swimming as fast as he could toward the dog. Mitch was a strong swimmer, but he couldn't quite get to it.

"Mitch, get out of there! You'll drown!" she cried, but she knew her brother. He would never give up. She looked around and found a large pile of driftwood. With all her might she heaved the largest one to Mitch, who caught it and used it to ease his fight against the undertow. With nearly the last strength he had in him, he was able to reach the dog—a chocolate lab, who had almost gone completely under and was coughing and choking. Mitch put the paws over his back and swam at a diagonal angle back to the shore.

• • •

"Lucy!!! Lucy!!!" Coach called and whistled, not caring that he may be disturbing the honeymooners and others in the posh villas. He ran and ran, calling her ceaselessly. When he saw the "No Swimming. Strong Undertow" sign, a lump the size of a baseball welled up in his throat, and he thought, "Oh no. Please no." Labs love the water, and Lucy was no exception. She never wandered off, but if there was a body of water nearby, it was a different story.

Just then, he observed the dramatic rescue followed by Mitch and Lucy lying exhausted in the warm sand. Amy had been crying, but after realizing both Mitch and the dog were okay, her tears turned to laughter. "Oh my God! You are so awesome!" She reached down to hug her brother.

"Yes, you are." A man's deep voice startled them. They all looked up to see a tall, fit man with good looks and a beige linen suit definitely not meant for the beach. Amy thought he might be a movie star.

Lucy managed to rise to all fours, sneezing, coughing, and shaking off the water like wet dogs do. She licked Coach like she hadn't seen him in years. Mitch caught his breath, and Amy was simply relieved it was all over.

"My villa is right over here," Coach said, "Let me get you kids some towels and something to drink."

After kudos and extreme expressions of gratitude, Coach passed out towels and bottles of water to everyone. As he dried Lucy, he thought about what a day it had been. He reached into his pocket to reward the kids $500 a piece, which was just a tenth of what he held in cash. Then he took his hand out of his pocket, almost ashamed of himself. These kids had just saved his best friend. They risked their own lives in doing so, and he was going to just hand them a few bills and send them on their way? No, he had to do more.

Coach, who was 42 years old, gave up private wealth and business coaching two years prior. He only took on a handful of very special clients, as he had worked intensely the past 25 years not just building the wealth and business coaching company, but amassing a great amount of money through several real estate and other business deals. His most famous mantra regarding being wealthy was, "Becoming a millionaire was my ultimate goal...until I became one."

He still wanted to coach, as he felt it was his duty to educate business owners and others sincerely wishing to know how to acquire true wealth, but he simply did not have the time for one-on-one sessions. So, he stuck to giving seminars every few months and publishing at least one book a year—all highly anticipated global best-sellers. "Richard Morgan, 'The Wealth Coach,'" was the J.K. Rowling of business books. Before digital books became *de rigueur*, people stood in line before the bookstores opened the day of each launch, eagerly awaiting their copy of his latest and greatest thoughts on finance and wealth.

His own children - Ashley, 10, Katie, 12, and Darnell, 14 - never had formal sessions with their father, but he coached them along the way, both by example and through impromptu discussions. He had never attempted to officially coach kids. He wondered if he was up for the challenge, and even more importantly, were these two youngsters? Would they even be interested?

Amy noticed the time. It was after eight o'clock. Their mother would be worried. "Sir?" she said sheepishly.

"Please, call me Coach. That's what my friends call me. And you are?"

"I'm Amy, and this is my brother, Mitch. May I please use your phone? Our mother doesn't know where we are, and we are supposed to meet her for dinner at The Bistro."

"Tell me what she looks like, and I'll do you one better than that," he said, picking up the desk phone. Amy quickly described her mother.

"Yes, Jean, there is a very attractive brunette..."

"Blonde!" Amy whispered louder than she meant.

"I'm sorry, blonde, named Kim, in an orchid-patterned dress waiting in The Bistro for her two teens, Mitch and Amy. Please find her, assure her that everything is okay, and escort her to my villa. Oh, and Jean, please order dinner for four, an assortment of whatever you think is appropriate for a celebration of two heroes."

"Mitch," Coach said, "why don't you go ahead and get showered off in the guest room? You and I are about the same size—I'll ring for the butler to set out some dry clothes for you."

Mitch, still more than a little exhausted, thought a shower and fresh clothes sounded like heaven. He knew he had seen that guy somewhere before. He was nice, *but who was he*? Whoever he was, he must have had *real* money to get this kind of service and accommodations.

Amy had managed to stay completely dry during the entire rescue, save for a few licks from Lucy. Now having the same sparkle in her big blue eyes that Coach was accustomed to seeing, she sat on the loveseat across from Coach as they waited for Jean to fetch Kim.

"Is your father also here?" Coach asked Amy.

Amy looked down, not really knowing what to say. She never considered Bryce her father, and she never knew her biological father.

Picking up on her discomfort, Coach scratched his chin and said, "Maybe we can discuss it later."

Mitch emerged from the guest room, looking quite dapper in Coach's resort shorts and polo shirt. "No, we'll tell you now," he said, almost angrily. This was the first time they'd spoken of it since Bryce died, leaving the family with nearly nothing. Mitch had forgotten about the lies he told about having life insurance and leaving them and their mother back at square one. Now his anger had bubbled to the surface, and something about Coach had made him feel comfortable enough to express it.

Amy was more realistic about the entire situation. In fact, shortly after Bryce died she had come to the realization that it wasn't just his fault for lying. It was also their mother's fault—for lying to herself and allowing herself to be ignorant about her family's finances. She even went so far, at least inside her own heart, to give him the benefit of the doubt for just trying to make everyone happy.

He sat next to Amy, with Lucy lying comfortably at Amy's feet as she scratched her between the ears. Mitch did all the talking, telling Coach the whole story about Bryce and their mother, how he had lied about their financial situation, the fateful night of their birthday, the whole nine yards.

"I see," Coach said sadly. He had heard plenty of hard-luck stories in his years, but this one was probably the most heart-wrenching.

"Yeah," Amy said, "most people staying here are *really* wealthy. We are *really* not! At all."

"You'd be surprised, Amy. Many people you see here—like you and your brother—simply *look* rich." He spoke reassuringly as he pulled a few pieces of the resort stationery from the desk and began to write something as he asked, "Mitch? Amy? Do you want to *look* wealthy, *be* wealthy—or both?"

The two looked at each other, as if the answer was a blinding flash of the obvious, and simultaneously answered, "Both!"

Then Mitch said, looking down at his borrowed ensemble, "Well, *really* being wealthy means you don't have to care. You can walk around looking like a bum one day and a king the next if you have millions. That would be cool!" They all got a laugh out of that one.

"Hey!" Mitch said, "I know who you are now. You are that 'Wealth Coach' guy on the signs in the lobby!"

Coach finished writing. "Yes, I am. The gigantic photos were not my idea, but I am 'The Wealth Coach,'" he said, sliding the paper towards the twins. He asked Amy to read it aloud. She read slowly, but with great enthusiasm.

I need a great big reason!
The only way I will achieve anything major is when I have a great big reason.

A WHY?

Burning in my head or my heart.

OR BOTH

"I want you to think for a minute about what you see on this page," Coach began. "I want you to tell me what you think is the significance of that statement."

Mitch pretended not to notice the frown on his sister's face. He tried to think for himself now without being influenced by what she might say, but he found his mind difficult to tame. He instinctively knew that the answers he thought of would not be the *right* ones, at least not according to Amy. He envisioned all sorts of things, like the plush surroundings and how cool it was that they were sitting at the table with "The Wealth Coach." He wondered if he would ever live that life of luxury.

"I guess it all has to do with motivation, Coach," Amy said after a long, thoughtful pause. "If there wasn't a reason to do something, why would anyone bother? Like, why would Mitch practice football two hours a day if he wasn't even on the team?"

Coach listened without replying. He didn't want to restrict either of their trains of thought.

"I, for one, always look for the easy option, Coach," Mitch chimed in, unabashed and eager to participate in the discussion. "I think it's best to conserve my energy and do things the easy way."

"Isn't that interesting?" Coach said after considering their replies. "Does that mean the easy way is always the better way, Mitch?"

"Not always, Coach. Sometimes there is no option but to take the long way. Like when you build a car, you have to do it step-by-step. There are no shortcuts."

"Consider this, then: are you not confusing the *process* of how to build a car with the *reasons* or motivation to do so? Why you'd want to build one in the first place? In other words, *not* 'Do I install the radiator before the catalytic converter?', but are you building a car because building cars is your hobby, or are you trying to save money? What is the *motivation* behind building the car?"

Mitch couldn't help blushing as he silently cursed his impetuous nature. He felt like an idiot.

"Don't feel stupid, ever," Coach quickly added in a reassuring voice. "You can speak your mind with me. Tell it like it is, or ask so-called *silly* questions. You see, I encourage you to think outside the square, push the boundaries, explore possibilities, and take chances. The only stupid questions are ones you don't ask."

Then Coach added, winking at Mitch, "And by the way, your analogy is correct. Building wealth is a step-by-step process."

Coach paused to let what he had said settle in with the twins. Mitch relaxed noticeably in his chair, thankful for Coach's understanding and sincerity.

Saved by the bell, Jean and Kim arrived, followed by three servers with huge silver platters. Jean's approaching Kim at The Bistro had been a little disconcerting, but she had only told her that "The Wealth Coach"—the man whose photo was on the signage in the lobby—had been chatting with the twins, and wanted them all to have dinner. The two women established an amicable rapport, and Kim had hoped they could hang out together sometime during the week.

Coach thanked and excused Jean while inviting Kim to sit at the table as a foursome - five if you counted Lucy, who slept peacefully under the table even as the waiters served dinner.

Confused, Kim finally asked, "Okay, what is this all about?"

Coach explained everything, as he thought of Kim and her situation. She certainly was a gorgeous woman. Though Coach truly had eyes for no one but his wife, he could see how a man like Bryce could end up trying to possess her and lose any hopes of true success in doing so. Many men did that with beautiful women, and she was *that* attractive. Plus, she did look rich. However, he knew better, and he felt a little guilty for putting her in his "Friday-night-rich" category. That is, someone who spends all their money to *look* rich instead of *be* rich. In other words, paid on Friday and broke by Monday.

Normally, Kim would have come unglued at hearing of Mitch fighting an undertow to rescue a dog, but she was strangely calm. Maybe it was that the twins seemed so contented, happy even, or perhaps it was Coach's soothing demeanor. Either way, she was joyful in the moment, and the dinner—a feast of lobster, steak, and exotic fruits and shellfish—was a lot better than the soup and salad she had planned to order at The Bistro.

"Mrs. Peters," Coach began.

"Please, call me Kim."

"Alright then, Kim. You have two fantastic children, and you must be a wonderful mother to have reared them so well," he said, very cautiously. "Your children saved my Lucy's life tonight. I know about your situation. The kids and I have been talking for some time—"

Suddenly, Kim was embarrassed, and she shot a displeased look at Amy.

"Please, Kim, don't be embarrassed or ashamed in any way. And don't be angry with Amy or Mitch. I pried it out of them, and that is a good thing. I believe that everything happens for a reason, and now, more than ever, I believe some universal force brought all of us together." He paused, thinking he sounded really corny. He wanted to blurt out his proposition—a gift that would truly repay the children for saving his cherished Lucy. He determined that in the short time they had spent together, the twins were not only coachable, but that they really needed it as well, as did their mother.

Coach offered Kim complimentary attendance to the seminar, but said that he would understand if she chose not to spend her vacation in a conference room. However, his most critical offer was for the twins: private coaching for an hour a day for the duration of the seminar.

After careful deliberation of what everyone wanted to do, the twins were eager to meet with Coach every day. He was cool, and if he could teach them to have what *he* had, to be like *him*, it might change the very trajectory of their futures.

"I want you both to understand that the coaching process is very different from the schooling process. With me, the only failure is the failure to participate. If you are up for the challenge, you can have a wonderful vacation and learn some life lessons that will propel you to great futures—futures that you design according to your dreams and visions."

He could tell by their earnest expressions that they needed no contemplation. "You must give this 100 percent, or we are just wasting our time. Are you in?"

A speechless Kim looked to the twins, who immediately answered, "Yes sir, Coach!" She herself needed to think overnight whether she would rather attend the seminar or take a much-needed break from reality. Coach understood Kim's dilemma, yet he knew that she would be doing both herself and her family a much bigger favor by attending the wealth seminar rather than lounging by the pool for a week drinking daiquiris.

"Kim, you think about it. I will have an itinerary sent to your suite. Mitch, Amy, I want you both to go to your suite now, take the paper I gave you, and think about our time together. I want you to pay particular attention to what your BIG reason is. Now I realize this may not be easy because you will find yourself thinking about all sorts of little reasons; they may seem like big ones on face value, but deeper reflection will reveal them to be temporary or short-term reasons. You'll understand what I mean when you begin thinking about this throughout our sessions. Lucy and I will meet you here tomorrow after dinner, say, seven o'clock?"

With everyone in agreement, Kim shook hands with Coach as the twins each spontaneously gave him a heartfelt, simultaneous hug. Lucy sat up, her tail wagging so hard, it actually made several loud thumps on the hardwood floor.

"We'll see you too!" Amy said, hugging Lucy. The three wandered back to their suite, which was still very nice, but not nearly as exquisite as Coach's villa.

It had definitely been an interesting and unexpected first day of their Hawaiian vacation.

Chapter 3

So Many Reasons, so Little Time

Kim couldn't sleep. Coach gave her much to think about. It was after one o'clock in California, so why couldn't she sleep? In her gut, she knew that she should attend the seminar. There would still be plenty of time to relax and unwind. Inside, though, she felt almost hopeless. She felt like it was too late for her, at the age of 44, to create a decent financial future for herself and the twins. She thought she had been doing that with Bryce, but she had only been kidding herself. Right now, all she could think about was getting out of debt and paying the monthly bills. Restless, she changed into some loungewear and took a walk around the resort, figuring she would have to get used to the time difference at some point.

Mitch and Amy stared at the ceiling fans above their comfy queen-sized beds. As the paddles rotated round and round, they both kept thinking about Coach and their BIG reasons.

"Remember, this is a fundamental question I have asked you," he had told them upon their leaving his villa. "Don't take it lightly. And I don't expect the final answer by tomorrow either. We will be talking more about why you'd want to be wealthy over the coming sessions, and this will all add up to helping you come up with a compelling reason why you really want—or should I say *choose*—to be wealthy."

They threw a few ideas around, but they seemed to be getting nowhere. This didn't concern Amy, as she kept remembering that Coach had said coming up with a BIG reason would probably take some time.

"To me," Mitch broke the silence, "being wealthy means I can always drive new cars, live wherever I want, travel to places like this whenever I feel like it, and always have enough money in the bank to finance it. Ooooh, and think about all the babes I could get!"

"Ugh!" Amy turned up her nose at the "babes" comment. She knew that cars, trips, or homes were not big enough reasons for choosing to be wealthy, and she made a point to resist the temptation of thinking the way her brother did. Even though she thought Mitch was on the wrong track, she didn't know if her reason for choosing wealth was clear enough. She liked the idea of being self-sufficient and independent throughout her life, never allowing herself to fall into the trap their mother had—depending on someone else for her and her family's financial security. She also dreamt of someday being able to contribute meaningfully to humanity, but she didn't know how she would go about doing that yet.

• • •

Kim saw the poster in the lobby and followed the directions to the classroom just to take a look. She was surprised to find Jean still in the room at nearly half past ten o'clock. She was doing one final checklist, making sure all attendees' collaterals were accounted for and in place.

"Hi Jean," Kim said softly, not wanting to startle her, "this is beautiful. Look at the flowers! And the linens—everything! You guys really worked hard on this, didn't you?"

Jean grinned and said, "It's a labor of love," as she checked off her final table. "I—and I'm sure Martin and Shaw too—have learned so much from attending Coach's seminars. It's like a bonus getting all this training, even though we are here as his event coordinators."

Kim noticed a tent card with her name on it on the table behind Jean. It read **Kim Peters** in bold letters, with a thick binder in front of it.

"Well," Kim said, "I guess I'll consider myself lucky that my kids saved your boss' dog - I get to have the training too." Now she was committed. It was only three hours a day for five days, which was hardly going to keep her out of her bikini and Hawaiian Tropic tanning oil the entire time. "And who knows," Kim thought, "I might learn of a way to finagle us out of this situation."

Kim noticed that Jean looked very tired, but she seemed proud of her work. She supervised Martin and Shaw, but really the team treated each other as equals. Kim talked Jean into one celebratory cocktail at the Lobby Bar, and Jean happily agreed to "just one."

The women sipped champagne with little orchid garnishes as the soft music of the ukulele strummed in the background. Kim told Jean her entire story, just as the twins had told Coach earlier. Jean revealed that she had a similarly humble—though not nearly as tragic—beginning when Coach came into her life as well. Jean patted Kim's hand in newfound friendship. "Don't worry. This is going to be really good for both you and the kids."

• • •

The twins heard their mother come in at half past midnight, which was really 4:30 in the morning in California. She saw the light on in their room, so she went in and noticed they were talking about Coach—something about a having a BIG reason to pursue a life of wealth.

Amy was the first to speak. "So mom, did you ever have a BIG reason to be wealthy?"

Amy's question made Kim think. When she had gone down to see the venue for the seminar, Jean was running a portion of a video from the previous seminar. Coach had begun his instruction in the video by telling the audience that there were three groups of people in the room when it came to being wealthy: those who never truly believed it would happen to them, those who thought it might be nice and hoped it would happen one day, and those who were committed to doing whatever it took to make wealth happen for them.

"Well you know, for many years I wanted to be rich. I thought about it, dreamed about it, hoped for it, talked about it, even read books and went to a seminar or two about it. I thought modeling would pay more, that I would be more of a supermodel, I guess. To be honest, part of why I married Bryce was that things had not panned out financially like I hoped. But, no, I never really had a real reason to be rich at all," she replied. "I just always kind of muddled through when your father left me with two babies to raise, thinking rich was something that happened to other people, not to me." She put her head down shamefully for a moment. "Then I thought I sort of saved us by marrying Bryce...but now, we are *really* starting over. I'm afraid that for your mama it's about making enough money to get out of this mess and get us back on track."

Mitch piped in, "So, maybe Bryce's dying and leaving us with almost nothing is a BIG reason? We *wanted* money before, but now we *need* it. Just to survive normally."

"Kids," their mother said, yawning, "you two have a great day tomorrow. Mitch, I saw you eyeballing that little gal in the pink bikini earlier," she winked. "You think about everything that coach says to you. I have to get some rest. I have a nine o'clock seminar to attend."

The twins beamed - they had hoped that their mom would choose to go to the seminar. They knew she was really looking forward to basking in the sun, relaxing by the pool, and taking a break from the whirlwind of reality cast upon them in the last few months. For the first time in a while, Mitch and Amy were actually proud of her.

...

After a day of swimming in the most awesome pool ever, with tons of waterfalls and hidden grottos—plus the cute girl with the pink bikini—Amy and Mitch grabbed some burgers at the pool grill, showered, and headed over to Coach's villa. They were a few minutes early, since he ran along the shoreline toward the twins, barefoot and shirtless in a pair of red shorts with Lucy at his side, whom they were glad to see safely on a leash.

"You're early!" Coach said, feeling particularly chipper after a great seminar and an invigorating run along the white sandy beach.

The twins, however, had mixed emotions. They were excited to talk to Coach again, but they felt worried about the lack of progress they had made with the homework he assigned.

"We can come back later," Amy said, hopefully.

"No, not at all," Coach replied, opening the door and motioning them to the dining table. "How did you do with your BIG reasons?" he asked as they took their seats.

"It was just as you said it would be, Coach," Amy replied. "We did a lot of thinking, and we talked a lot, but we didn't get very far."

As Coach unleashed Lucy and fed her, he said, "That's okay. I just wanted you to begin thinking, that's all. But that's not the end of this topic of reasons. You see, there is more to it than that."

The twins were relieved.

"I'm going to take a quick shower," Coach sad. He pulled another piece of hotel stationary from the desk quickly writing the following words:

"Now you two ponder this while I rinse off, and we'll discuss it in a moment," Coach instructed as he disappeared down the hall.

Mitch took the paper, read it silently to himself twice over, and handed it to Amy. The words perplexed Amy this time. For once, it was Mitch who seemed to have the answer.

"I think I see what Coach is getting at, Amy," he said. "It's like football—I can be running away from a tackler and towards the goal line at the same time, both negative and positive goals right? That makes a whole lot of sense."

Amy agreed, "I think I get it now."

Coach overheard Mitch's explanation as he emerged down the hallway, toweling his hair dry. "Good, Mitch," he said. "Negative reasons can be very, very powerful. They can actually be more powerful than positive reasons. For instance, my wife is a diet and exercise fanatic because her mother struggled with obesity her entire life, and she doesn't want to look like that or have her health issues."

"So, Coach?" Amy asked, "If my mom wants to be wealthy, is her BIG reason based on a negative one because she told us last night all she wants to do is get us out of this mess and not be broke again. Does it mean *she* is negative or that she can't succeed?"

"Amy, most people have no trouble deciding what they *don't* want in life, finding negative motivators—things to move away from," Coach explained. "Your mother doesn't want the pain of the debt your family is currently in, and she doesn't want your family to be broke. Just because it is a negative reason does not mean it is a bad one. However, it does probably mean, let's hope, that it is a temporary reason."

Mitch was itching to contribute to the discussion, "That's a strong motivator that my football coach uses on us all the time. He constantly reminds us that unless we turn up for practice every day and take it seriously, we will never be the best. And I think I'm pretty good—that our whole team is."

Coach was pleased with his new students - they caught on quickly.

"So now that you know that there are such things as negative reasons to want to be wealthy, let's take a look at how negative reasons affect the motivation to choose wealth,"he said as he wrote on another piece of paper:

My negative reasons
WHY
are short-term motivators.
Most people start with a negative reason - to prove something to someone, to get out of debt. Or to quit a bad job or relationship. Basically, I may want to get out of some sort of pain, but that will generally only
MOTIVATE ME
short term.

"That's really interesting, Coach," Amy said after reading the page. "It makes so much sense to me. Mom wants to be wealthy, but her negative reason is to get out of the pain of being broke."

Mitch, too, was excited by this new information. It gave him a sharper insight into both the motivation of his family's situation as well as how and why his football coach used negative reasons.

"With football, we are only talking about one game at a time. It now makes more sense as to why our coach would better motivate us by showing how each game contributes to the larger picture."

"Exactly," Coach replied, speaking as he scrawled quickly on another piece of paper. "What effect do you think it would have if he were to keep using these negative motivators—avoid being tackled, don't lose the game—but then add some positive reasons? Which, as you may have guessed, are longer-term motivators? Performance would be more than just about one game - now, it spans a whole season. Speaking of positive goals, have a read of this next sheet."

He handed them the next sheet, which Mitch read aloud:

> My positive reasons why are longer-term motivators. Generally, most people never make the transition
>
> **TO POSITIVE WHYs.**
>
> Once they are out of pain, they stop. Average is okay for them. I need to find a reason to move from average to pleasure, so
>
> **I KEEP MOVING**
>
> long-term with positive reasons.

Coach sat in silence to allow the twins to absorb this new information. He addressed his next question to Mitch. "What do you think the result would have been, Mitch, if your football coach had said...wait, what is the name of your team?"

"The Mavericks," Mitch said with pride.

Coach continued, "What if your coach said, 'The Mavericks must strive to be remembered as the greatest team the entire division has ever seen, a hundred years from now?' Do you think that would have been a compelling reason for you to train hard and play games that people will still be talking about for years to come?"

"Well I guess it would have some impact, but most of my team really couldn't care less as long as they get to play each week," Mitch replied.

"So who would use positive reasons then, Coach?" Amy asked.

"Professional athletes, for one, Amy. Presidents and other national leaders would as well. Business people who have a great vision for both their businesses and themselves also use positive reasons. It's not about being average. It's about being the best."

Amy made a few notes down the side of her page, and then continued: "But how would ordinary people like us use positive reasons, Coach? I mean, we would hardly be worried about how things are a hundred years from now, would we Mitch?"

He shook his head in agreement.

Coach was particularly happy that Amy not only took notes, but that she had rewritten in nice, almost calligraphic handwriting the statements he had jotted down on the hotel stationery. He always believed that writing things down, not just typing or trying to remember, greatly reinforced learning.

"In your case your timeframe might not be quite so long, Amy. However, you could still take a long view - like what you want to happen by the time you retire. Now I know that normally at your age you'd hardly give your retirement a second thought, but this is something you are going to have to change if you really want to start building wealth. You really do need to think that far ahead."

She nodded in understanding.

"Now let me give you one last sheet for this session," Coach said as he slid them another sheet of paper.

I've only got one shot –

ONE LIFE.

That is approximately
4.000 weeks to do the best I can.
Why would I want to waste
it being less than I can be?
I need to make the most of
the gift of life and be the

BEST ME I can be.

Some people didn't get that
gift today.

Mitch whistled softly as he finished reading. He nodded and looked at Amy.

"You know, that's one of the coolest things I've ever read," he said, noticeably moved. Coach didn't say a thing. He knew the power of silence.

"You *do* learn something new every day," Coach said. "When you think about it, we're all well into our 4,000 weeks already, aren't we? I mean, how much time have we already used up?"

Amy scribbled quickly with her pencil. "Sixteen years times 52 weeks equals...832 weeks. Wow, that is nearly a quarter of a lifetime. So that means we roughly have 3,168 weeks left of our lives."

Coach, pleased his students were taking a genuine interest in their sessions, kept the momentum going. "The ultimate point here is that if the average lifespan is 4,000 weeks or 77 years, we really owe it to ourselves and our world to make the most of the time we are given—not to squander our existence."

They both nodded in agreement.

"So just to drive the point home, you must understand that once time has passed it is gone forever, regardless of how we spent it."

"Right, Coach," Mitch said, excitedly. "It's like in football - we only have so many minutes of play to win the game. That is the time we have, and it is up to us as a team to make the most of it."

Coach noticed that Mitch always used sports analogies. It was something he understood and to which he could relate.

"So remember," he said with finality, "No matter how you spend your time, it will pass and be gone forever. There is no rewind button in life."

Amy felt she had gained a whole new perspective on life from Coach's words. Maybe it was her youth, but she had never realized the importance of the aspect of time and how one spends it.

"Then," Coach went on, "what is the significance of time and how it relates to life? We cannot change the past, but we can certainly influence the future by taking actions that are positive. Time will go by no matter what, but you can choose whether to make a positive decision or a negative decision with that time." He paused. "And when you think about it, it takes the same amount of energy to make a positive decision as it does to make a negative one."

Coach made sure to explain to the twins the difference between positive and negative reasons and positive and negative decisions.

After reviewing her notes she patted Lucy, who always seemed to be listening intently to Coach's wisdom just as the twins did. Amy summed up the lesson perfectly: "I guess a positive decision is one that takes us closer to our goals, while a negative one does not. In fact, it could even bring us further from them."

Coach was very pleased with the progress made by his two newest students, and he silently congratulated himself for his decision to reward them with knowledge rather than to simply give them money for saving Lucy's life. He, better than anyone, understood the old Chinese proverb: Give a man a fish, and you feed him for a day. Teach a man to fish, and you feed him for a lifetime.

"Younger people certainly seem to make more promising students," Coach thought to himself. "They are like little sponges for knowledge, while many older people think they already know it all even though their results show that they have neither applied nor used anything they say they know." He wondered how Kim would respond to his same lessons in a classroom setting.

"I want you to think about what we have discussed today and to reevaluate last night's homework in light of it. See you both tomorrow?"

The twins nodded as they made their way to the pool. They were hoping their mother was there so they could talk to her about their session and find out how the seminar went.

Along the way, Mitch noticed the cute girl in the pink bikini. Except this time the pink one was white with little flowers. He wanted to say something to her. Not only was she beautiful, with an athletic body and flowing black hair, but both times he saw her she seemed like such a happy, confident young woman. He had actually caught her eye as she gave him a little grin before getting up and diving into the pool.

"Mitch," Amy said, "You are such a babe-hound. Look, there's mom."

"Hi mom," Amy said.

"Kids!" Kim squealed, hugging both of them like she hadn't seen them in weeks. She always did that. Amy thought it was sweet, while Mitch thought his mom was completely spastic. "OH MY GOD! Coach's class was AMAZING!!!"

Kim hadn't yet eaten dinner, and Mitch and Amy were always hungry, so they sat down at a table together to discuss the day. Amy looked out past the resort, over the horizon of the foamy white and indigo surf, to a spectacular full moon and thought about how perfect the moment was. She made a silent vow that no matter what, she would use Coach's sessions to create the very life she desired, even if her mom and Mitch ever lost interest, as both tended to do with anything that wasn't 100 percent exciting or easy.

However, she hoped for the best, and she hoped that they would stay with it as she promised herself she would.

"So mom, do you think you have positive or negative goals?" Mitch asked, completely catching her off guard.

"Have you already talked about that with Coach in your session? We spent most of the day on goals, and..." She paused for a moment, not really sure how much to go into, but she pressed on.

"My goals when I was with Bryce, and even now, were and are negative. I wanted to escape being broke when I married him. I always dreamed of being wealthy, but I never really thought I would be. It's not the only reason I married him, but I definitely think I settled because I knew he could get me out of living paycheck-to-paycheck. And I spoke with Coach a bit at break, and he told me that currently trying to get out of debt and avoid being broke are indeed negative goals, but that it is okay for now. Ensuring that you two get to graduate from your school and my being able to acquire enough to put you through college are positive goals, and my goals and reasons for being wealthy will probably expand over the years, becoming bigger and more positive."

Amy spoke again as Mitch sat quietly. "What do you mean you always dreamt of being rich, but never thought you really would, mom?"

"Yes, honey, but dreaming about and hoping to be wealthy is different from really believing it, going for it, learning how and actually coming up with a goal and a plan for it. Coach really taught us the difference today in class. Only when we have real goals, positive goals, and BIG goals do we actually need to start learning about wealth and really planning for it."

The twins were still struggling with this concept of goals and wealth, but knowing that even adults had a hard time with it, made it seem okay to be a little overwhelmed.

Kim, pleased they seemed to be taking their coaching sessions seriously, knew this wasn't something the average 16-year-old did. But then again, these weren't ordinary 16-year-olds, she reasoned. Coach had told her that he, too, was pleased with their progress. He predicted that they would grow up to be really strong people, and this made her proud. As for Kim, these early days of setting goals and deciding on being more than average were going to be hard for her, and she knew that the kids must have been working hard on it too. At least they had the advantage of starting at a younger age.

She knew that they were thankful for being given the opportunity to learn about taking control of their financial lives so early on. She also hoped that they were taking the time to have some fun during the day. She knew they were spending a lot of time talking about their sessions. She could hear them talking at night, and Amy always had her notebook with her, whether at the pool, the beach, or the restaurant. Kim was surprised she didn't take it surfing with her!

Amy found that in just two short days and two hours of face time with Coach, her mind couldn't stop racing. Most people would probably feel overwhelmed by the sheer amount of concepts and exercises Coach had given, but it actually excited her. She couldn't wait for the time when she and her brother would begin doing something practical as far as actually creating wealth was concerned. She wouldn't just think and research, but do! However, as Coach had pointed out a few times: there is no use doing something until you know what to do and why you are doing it.

Chapter 4

CHANGES

The next day Kim eagerly prepared for the seminar, showing up a few minutes early in case Jean needed any help. She really liked Jean, and could tell that Coach relied mainly on her to execute these fantastic events.

Jean sat behind a table in front of the meeting room. It was stacked with all of Coach's books and brochures. Something looked wrong. "Are you okay, Jean?" Kim asked, startling her a bit. "I hate to say it, but you don't look well."

Jean made a disgusted face."Oh, Kim! Can you watch the table for just a second?" she asked, running across the hall to the ladies' room. She emerged minutes later, wiping her brow with a cloth.

"Did you get sick?" Kim asked, incredulously.

Jean closed her eyes and nodded. "I'm two weeks late," she sighed.

"Late?" Kim asked, at first confused. Then as Jean touched her belly, Kim got the hint. "Oh, I see...do Mr. and Mrs. Patterson have a little one on the way?"

"Well, either that or the shellfish I ate last night was bad."

Kim laughed. "Well, you'd better find out," she said with a raised eyebrow. "We'll go to the sundries shop when class is over. In the meantime, maybe you should explain to Coach that you are feeling a bit ill. I am available to sit in the back in case you have to leave unexpectedly."

The seminar went extremely well, and Jean only had to excuse herself twice, leaving Kim to pass out some worksheets and collect homework assignments. Directly after the seminar, the women headed to the sundries shop.

...

Meanwhile, Mitch and Amy spent the morning surfing, not really talking too much about the sessions. Mitch couldn't get his mind off the girl with the long black hair, and Amy couldn't stop contemplating about her BIG reason. She thought that maybe a little surfing would clear her mind, but it just rejuvenated her, giving her more and more possible BIG reasons for following Coach's instructions and *choosing* wealth. She really needed to explore what was important to her, and she remembered that Coach said it would take time - their reasons may even change throughout life.

Amy was slightly irritated that Mitch didn't seem as enthused as she was with the sessions. They got to "play" all day, and this was the opportunity of a lifetime. It wasn't that Mitch was disinterested; he eagerly attended the sessions, and they had many productive discussions, but he seemed distracted. When they did talk about the BIG reasons, positive and negative decision making, positive and negative reasons for choosing a life of wealth over one of mediocrity, or worse, poverty, his were always about being rich just to be rich. Just so he could buy cars, homes, travel...all things she wanted too, but she felt she had a better grasp on Coach's conveyances than did Mitch. She wanted him to be as introspective as she was.

As she caught her last wave, she noticed that Mitch was talking to someone in the distance. It was the girl with the black hair. Amy decided to cut Mitch a little slack - the girl seemed very confident and friendly whenever they passed each other on the beach or by the pools. She decided she would go say hello, promising herself that she would not embarrass her brother, and take some time to go snorkeling for the afternoon.

The girl's name was Nancy, and she was every bit as nice as Amy thought she would be.

She asked the concierge when the next charter sailed, and luckily there was one boarding at noon and arriving back to shore at four o'clock. This would give her plenty of time to eat, study, shower, and get to their session. Originally, she had hoped Mitch would go snorkeling with her. They had made a deal where she would try parasailing if he would go snorkeling. Now her main concern was that Mitch wouldn't lose interest in their sessions now that he finally hooked up with his dream girl.

Amy, relieved the excursion was already prepaid, quickly picked up her beach bag and headed to the dock. The catamaran sailed to a rocky cove, where the guide said many fantastic sea creatures "hung out." Then, he gave instructions as he put on scuba gear and followed his snorkeling passengers as they dove into the turquoise water.

She didn't know which direction to go. There were so many choices: ahead, there was a cavern that seemed a little scary. To her left were the shallower waters where she could examine the corals and sea urchins, clams and oysters. To her right was a school of tiny silver fish that appeared to be nipping at two fellow snorkelers as they swam through the school. Or, she could simply keep drifting ahead at the top until something interesting compelled her to dive under and examine. Suddenly the guide emerged, seemingly from nowhere, holding a puffer fish. Puffer fish, she had read, only puffed out when frightened, and this one definitely was. The guide motioned for her to touch it, but as she reached out, he pointed to the beak-like mouth and shook his head, warning her not to touch there.

As she felt the fish's rough skin while the guide held the fish in place, she thought of Coach and the homework assignment he had given the twins. She thought about the positive and negative reasons for wealth, positive and negative decisions, and the average time humans had to create their vision, their wealth—or not.

As she rose to the surface to catch her breath, she thought of the array of choices she could have made in just the last few minutes. She could have ignored the guide and touched the beak, possibly getting her finger bitten off. She could have felt what it was like to be nipped at by an entire school of fish— she later found out from the other snorkelers that they tickled and didn't hurt at all. She could have ventured into the cavern where she spied the dangerous eel. Alternatively, she could have stayed on the catamaran as some did, never getting into the water, instead lying in the hot sun drinking punch and having sandwiches. Or, she could have chosen not to go at all and never had this experience.

The hours went by too quickly. She had experienced so much in such a short time. She now knew the vastness of the ocean, what a puffer fish felt like, and how beautiful all of the reef fish looked up close. As she basked in the sun on the return trip, she kept in mind the analogous nature of her day's experiences with what Coach had said about decisions. She made many in a few short hours, all somewhat life-changing, but not nearly as life-changing as the ones Coach asked Mitch and Amy to ponder. No wonder he told them this wealth coaching experience would take time. Building a vision and creating wealth would be a process they would engage in over time—years.

As she basked in the warmth of the tropical sun, she kept meditating on one of Coach's mantras: "There is no use in doing something until you know what to do and why you are doing it."

• • •

Well, Mitch knew exactly what he was doing when he and Nancy found a hidden grotto in the resort pool. It was vast, but not nearly as vast as the ocean he had yet to experience the way Amy had. She saw that there was a hidden grotto, but no eel there—just two young kids experiencing puppy love, smooching and holding hands with not another soul in sight. They talked and talked for hours, though it seemed like minutes. Unfortunately, she lived clear in Texas, but was considering college in California. She just didn't know where. Like him, she was interested in sports—especially football. In fact, she was captain of the cheerleading squad, which, Mitch figured, explained the amazing athletic body.

It was only when the small opening at the top of the grotto revealed a dimming sky did Mitch remember his session with Coach and Amy, as well as the homework he had given them. He remembered how Coach told them from the beginning that he must give this time they had together 100 percent or nothing.

"Nancy, I have to go meet my sister," he said, trying to keep his cool. He gave her one last kiss on the cheek and said, "Come on," taking her hand and swimming out of the grotto.

He and Amy arrived at Coach's door at the same time, just a few minutes before seven o' clock. They didn't have time to argue. Coach opened the door before they knocked. "Amy," Coach smiled, "you look particularly lovely this evening," then he turned to Mitch. "And Mitch..." he paused a bit as he assessed Mitch's disheveled appearance, "it's always good to see you."

Embarrassed, Mitch pulled out a dry towel from his bag, set it on the chair and sat at the table, ready or not, for their session. He was relieved that Coach went right into the next lesson and didn't ask about the homework... yet. This time, the pages were already written out and photocopied, so they each had their own. Coach wanted to see if Amy would still make her own colorful one later.

"Make sure all your actions are ones you'll be proud of," Coach said. "They will, after all, bear your signature. If you think about how you'd like to be remembered after you are dead and gone, these are the types of actions I'm talking about."

> My actions earn me my reputation.
> **I WANT**
> my epitaph to read, "I gave everything my absolute best."
> When my life
> **IS OVER,**
> imagine how proud people will feel about me. This is the sort of life I want to have.

He took a long pause and looked at each twin square in the eyes. "Wealth is important, but it's not something to ever lose respect over."

Mitch could relate. In fact, he wondered if Coach somehow knew how he had spent his afternoon. "But was it wrong?" he silently wondered. He couldn't take it anymore. He had to discuss Nancy with Coach and Amy.

"Coach, I have to tell you something," he said. "I haven't really given last session's homework a second thought until now. See," he said blushing, "I met a girl today."

Coach looked at Amy, "And Amy what did you do today?"

"Okay, I admit that I took the day to surf and snorkel. But I did do my homework, and everything fell into perspective..."

Coach cut her off. "I'm sure it did, Amy. Look kiddos, I told you this process would take time. Never did I ask you to not have fun or not enjoy your friends or have a social life. I am simply asking you to start setting goals and build a vision for your futures. Get ahead of the game, but don't give up the precious moments of your youth."

Mitch was thankful that Coach reiterated his intent that this would be a years-long journey, and that he wanted them to go about their routines and enjoy their youth. He only asked that they give extra special consideration to their futures.

Amy was a bit put off that time was almost up, and she hadn't yet had the chance to share her epiphany about the vastness of the ocean, the choices, the reasons...

While Amy was happy for her brother and his new girlfriend, she felt a little neglected. The twins had always hung out together. Now someone else was taking her best friend's place. *She* didn't want a vacation fling. But then again, there were so many interesting things to do on the island, and besides, she could make a positive decision to be just a little more focused than her brother on the sessions. This was a gift she was not going to diminish.

"Good session, guys. You really seem to be getting it, and we haven't even touched the tip of the iceberg. And speaking of this session, I'm afraid I will have to cut it a bit short. Your mother and my assistant, Jean, need to meet with me. Just keep pondering. We will continue with this discussion about our actions and reputations tomorrow."

All of them agreed. The twins walked back to their suite, and Coach got dressed to meet Kim and Jean at the lobby bar.

• • •

Right after the seminar Kim found a pregnancy test, paid for it, and met Jean back outside while she rested on a bench next to "Charles," a blue-fronted Amazon parrot. Many considered the bird to be the resort's most clever comedian. He kept saying, "What are you doing? What are you doing?" She felt a bit better, but was tired and somewhat clammy.

"Come on, let's do this," Kim commanded. She took Jean by the arm up to her room, which was quite small compared to Kim's luxury suite.

A few minutes later Jean emerged from the restroom and nodded, smiling and crying tears of joy. Kim squealed her little happy squeal and hugged Jean tightly.

Jean explained that she wanted to remain loyal to Coach, but she really wanted to spend some time taking care of herself during pregnancy in preparation to be a full-time mom.

"Well," Kim lit up, "it just so happens that I am looking for a job. I would love to work with Coach and fill in for you, even if it's only temporary while you take some maternity leave. You said his main office was in Calabasas... that is only 40 minutes from my house."

Jean smiled in relief. She knew that Kim was more than competent enough to do the job, and that Coach would love staying in touch with their family. In the short time he had taken on Mitch and Amy, he had not only found them very coachable, but it gave him a whole new perspective on how he might coach his own children.

Jean and Kim arrived first. "I guess this means no more champagne cocktail hours for us," Jean said, smirking.

"Hey, I'm not the one who's preggers!" Kim said, feigning sarcasm. Yet out of solidarity, she ordered a sparkling apple cider along with Jean as they waited for Coach.

When he arrived, shortly after Kim and Jean got their "mocktails," he ordered a beer and asked what was going on. It was with mixed emotions that he agreed to hire Kim while Jean took some time off. On one hand, Kim needed the job, and he was hopeful she could do it. On the other hand, Jean had been with him five years and did amazing work. What if Kim wasn't as good?

"Well," Coach raised his glass for a toast, "to your good news, Jean, and to my new assistant, Kim."

Coach stuck around the bar after the two women left. He never thought until now about how he was going to continue coaching Mitch and Amy after the seminar was over. Certainly five days was not going to be long enough. However, now that he knew of their close proximity, coaching them over time would be a lot easier. All in all, he was happy for Jean, as he knew she had desperately wanted a baby. He just hoped Kim could do the same stellar job Jean did for him.

Chapter 5

The Long Haul

"We are going to carry on from where we left off last night," Coach said once they had taken their seats around the table. "Before we go on, let's review what you kiddos got out of last night's shortened session."

"Basically," Amy said, "make sure all our actions are ones we'll be proud of."

"That's right, Amy," Coach added. "Your actions will, after all, bear your signature. If you think about how you'd like to be remembered after you're dead and gone, those are the types of actions I'm talking about. Wealth is important, but again, it's never something to lose respect over."

Mitch could relate to this.

"It's a lot like how well-behaved sportsmen are remembered, isn't it, Coach?" he said. "I mean, they are always remembered for the great things they did on the playing field, aren't they? Like the records they set, the goals they scored and the teams they played for."

Coach applauded Mitch's analogy, but asked him to go further. "What else though? Are *all* great athletes well remembered, and *only* for their athletic careers?"

Mitch and Amy both thought a moment. Amy, at a loss because she wasn't really a sports fan, thought it was funny how Mitch always thought in terms of sports.

Mitch thought for a moment. Then, in a flash of what he felt was genius, piped up, "Lou Gehrig, the great baseball player! He played in six World Series champion teams and was the first Major League Baseball player to have his uniform number retired, plus he held a bunch of other records."

"Go on..." Coach could see Mitch got it.

"But he also got sick and voluntarily took himself out of the game. He died two years later, but they have an award in his name, The Lou Gehrig Memorial Award, which they give once a year to the Major League Baseball player who shows the most integrity and character."

Coach was pleased. "Remarkable. Now, can either of you think of a famous athlete who set great records and received awards, but is remembered for other, more dubious actions?"

Amy actually knew the answer to this one. She remembered a football player who Bryce, when he was alive, was shocked had died suddenly. "It turned out," she said, "that he was one of the best quarterbacks in the NFL ever, but he ended up getting caught cheating on his wife all the time and abusing her physically. Eventually, he finally disappeared from the NFL. I think he ended up in jail or something."

"That's right, Amy. Sad story," Coach said. "Remember, it's not just great sports stars that are remembered by their actions. We do the same with great business people, adventurers, generals, politicians, entertainers, and almost anyone else who is at the forefront of their particular field."

Mitch couldn't help thinking how natural this all felt. He instinctively knew that it was also making sense to Amy. And that, to him, was the beauty of coaching. It just seemed like common sense, but somehow Coach put it in an order that he could see as being a natural progression toward something greater.

Coach then handed the twins their two sheets of paper. He was pleased to notice that Amy had inserted into her binder the one from the previous night's session in her own colorful writing.

Mitch, unprompted, read his aloud:

My only job in life is to be the best me that I can be. I have been given a certain set of talents and skills, and **I HAVE NO RIGHT** but to be the best I can be and to use my talents and skills to be the best I can, because that's how **I AM DESIGNED.**

"Too many people live their lives without truly ever being their best. No matter what job you have, you need to do and be your best," Coach explained. "If you were the best version of *you*, you would be healthy, wealthy, and have great relationships. Life would necessarily be great," Coach said, satisfied that his two new students had truly digested and understood the words on the page. He continued, with even greater intensity, "*Everything* you do is about being your best. Every decision, every action. Remember, life is not a dress rehearsal—it's a gift, and with that gift comes the responsibility of giving everything your best shot."

The twins couldn't believe how adamant Coach felt about this particular point. In fact, he stood up and pointed at them.

"One of our defining characteristics as human beings is our ability to choose," he said. "In fact, this need to choose is pretty fundamental, especially where wealth is concerned. You see, we have no choice but to choose: wealth, middle class, or poverty. I want you to think long and hard about what I have just said. *We have no choice but to choose.*"

The room fell into silence as the twins began thinking about what they had just learned. Then, after a long, thoughtful pause, Amy spoke. "I'm not sure if I am on the right track here, Coach, but does this mean we cannot choose *not* to choose?"

"That's it, Amy," Coach smiled widely, clapping his hands together. "We have to choose, whether we like it or not. Think of it this way—if we choose not to choose, we've still made a choice, right?"

"That's kind of scary, Coach," she said, still deep in thought.

"And it really does take the same amount of effort to choose right or wrong, good or bad, wealthy or poor, best or average. So why not choose that which is in your best interest? Now before we conclude tonight's session, there's one more handout I'd like you two to think about." He handed them each a piece of paper.

I must add value.
The more value I add to the world, the more the world
REWARDS ME.
The more I serve, the more
I DESERVE.

"One of the best pieces of advice I can give you is this: always add value to whatever you do. That way you will be rewarded, and one of the rewards that you will eventually achieve is wealth. Be diligent, smart, persistent, conscientious, and creative. Add value. This way, you will be sure to leave the world a better place than you found it."

Coach leaned back in his chair, ran his hands through his short, cropped dark hair, took in a deep breath and then relaxed.

"If you were to really think about it, it's by adding value to something that you make both your mark and your money. It's usually what you do with something or how you improve it. How you add value to something determines how much you make."

"So Coach," Amy asked, "are you saying that it could be as simple as picking up a piece of trash someone littered on the beach?"

He could see that they were following what he said.

"Or is it as difficult—but rewarding—as training for a marathon? Adding value is what's at the core of wealth creation."

Mitch could feel himself getting excited now, but he didn't quite understand what picking up litter or running a marathon had to do with creating wealth.

"You see, if you invest some money, it's how you invest it that will determine the result you get. Invested poorly, it will bring in, at best, poor results; you may even lose. But invested wisely, it will return you great results."

Mitch shifted around in his chair and said, "Coach, I'm really excited about understanding how to go about creating wealth, but what are we talking about here? I mean, is it something we can just do and get great results, or am I missing something?"

Coach pondered the question for a moment, not wanting to give the wrong answer due to a misunderstanding.

"Kiddos, it's not a get-rich-quick type of thing, if that's what you mean. Take gambling, for instance. Of course many people can enjoy it, afford it, and control it. But if all you had was, say, $1,000, would it be wise to 'invest' it in a single hand of blackjack or spin of the roulette wheel?"

"Only if we won!" Amy said jokingly.

Coach wasn't amused.

"Mitch and Amy, I aim to coach you over a considerable length of time because building wealth is a long-term thing. It's a life-long approach, something that involves more than just learning a few strategies and ideas. It's more about changing your habits, changing the way you view life, and possibly even the world from here on out. It's all about understanding these basic principles and applying them to everything you do during the course of your lives."

"But Coach," Mitch said, somewhat deflated, "your trip ends in just three days, how can you keep coaching us?"

It was the perfect moment to tell the twins about what he had discussed with their mother and Jean the night before.

"You mean your house is that close to our house?! And mom has a job with you now?!" Amy's eyes lit up brightly.

Coach grinned ever so slightly, "Well Amy, *one* of my homes is in Calabasas, as is my main office, so yes, we got lucky there. Keep in mind, though, my family and I have several residences all over the world. Plus, I still have my seminars to give. But yes, our close proximity will allow me to coach you. Not as frequently as before, but as much as necessary for years to come." He then patted Lucy, who was lying at his feet, and nodded to the twins, almost as a reminder of how their relationship began.

"You see, creating wealth starts with learning, and learning takes time. Then there is the doing, and that also takes time. Then the market cycles must move with you. This takes time as well. They all move together, but some adults come to me wanting to get rich in a year or two, when the reality is it takes about ten years to learn, apply and benefit from real wealth strategies and principles."

This was just what Mitch wanted to hear. His mom had always told him that if something seemed too good to be true, it probably was. This always stuck in his head, and he finally felt absolutely sure he wasn't getting tied up with something that fell into that category.

"Well, that just about wraps things up for today. We have two more sessions together here on Maui. It is time to finalize—at least for now—your own BIG reasons for wanting to be wealthy. If you truly can't think of one yet, by all means talk to your mother and talk to me, but really try to think for yourselves. You may need to go home and put all you've learned into perspective before you come up with your BIG reason. This is what is going to motivate you over the months and years ahead, especially when times get tough and it becomes difficult to see light at the end of the tunnel."

He shook hands with his young students and walked with them to join their mother at The Bistro. He knew she was proud of them and their diligent attitudes, and he wanted to congratulate her for rearing two amazing young adults. He also wanted to set a date to sit down with her and discuss the details of the coming job, such as the starting date, job description, salary, et cetera.

"I've given them some very important homework to do," he said, as much to the twins as to their mother, "so we will meet tomorrow and possibly Friday. I want them to do some soul-searching now and to come up with real BIG reasons as to why they want to become wealthy."

The three decided to wait until their first session in California to revisit their BIG reasons. One session remained, and Coach wanted to spend it with Kim. As the twins' mother, his new employee, and a woman young enough to still build wealth (though it would be a tough go), he felt he needed to work some things out with her. The twins agreed to make sure she would be there at seven o'clock the following night.

Kim nervously headed to Coach's villa. She didn't know why she felt nervous. She knew him for less than a week, yet it felt like they were old friends. And for someone so successful, he was one of the most down-to-earth, unpretentious men she had ever met, but now he would be her boss. Would it change the game?

Coach welcomed her in, and once she saw Lucy resting after her evening run and the warm welcome in Coach's eyes, she instantly felt at ease.

"Kim, I asked for you here because I think we should talk about *your* financial situation," he said cautiously.

She took a gulp of her wine, a bigger one than she had planned.

"Don't get me wrong. You were left in a horrible position..."

"Well," she said, thinking about some things she learned at the seminar, "I have to take responsibility for allowing that to happen. I chose not to be involved. I chose to be ignorant."

Coach was glad she admitted it herself and that he didn't have to point it out. One thing Coach didn't buy into was blaming others for the situation you are in. This was her first big step.

"So," he went on, "we've talked about BIG reasons, little reasons, positive reasons, negative reasons, decisions...so much, with the twins and in class. Kim, let's decide right now how you are going to move on from this negative reason you have for gaining wealth—to get out of debt—and turn it positive so that you don't get stuck with *average* once you are out of debt and living in reasonable comfort once again."

Kim wanted to cry. She had been able to ignore the financial situation in which she now found herself, but she wasn't looking forward to going home and dealing with it all.

"Now you purchased a home in Oxnard for approximately 300,000 dollars, and that's a modest home."

Kim nodded, wondering where this was going.

"In seminar, we discussed cash flow, physical assets, and paper assets. The twins and I are nowhere near this level in our coaching. However," and Coach tried to say this delicately, "you and I are about the same age, I would guess..."

"I'm 44 years old," Kim said. She was not one to be ashamed of her age.

Relieved by her candor, Coach continued. "Amy and Mitch have the benefit of starting their real wealth building in their teens. You are essentially starting over at 44. I always say that when starting from square one it will take about ten years to build your wealth, but you *can* do it, Kim."

Kim felt relieved, overwhelmed, and a little confused at the same time.

"You actually did a good thing by buying a modest, older home. And now, you will now be generating active income with your job," Coach said, trying never to sound condescending, just treating her like a peer. "There are a few things we need to go over, though, if you are truly going to become wealthy."

Kim tried hard not to seem too wide-eyed, but she was mesmerized at the thought that she was sitting before a truly wealthy man who was going to teach her his secrets for getting rich...hopefully sooner rather than later.

Almost as if he had read her mind, he wrote something down and handed it to her.

> There are no get-rich-quick-schemes. This is why **PEOPLE** who win the lottery are usually **BROKE** in just a year or two.

Kim, feeling a combination of confusion and disappointment, wasn't quite sure what to do with the paper.

Coach noticed her hesitation, but kept going for a few minutes. He wanted to assess how committed she was to attaining wealth. She certainly didn't have the eager attitudes of her children, but then, he thought, maybe she was just a bit out of gas.

"Kim, listen," he said definitively, "the reason this process takes time is because you have to learn before you earn. In other words, getting wealthy is mostly about learning how to make money, and that takes time."

"But I..." she started to protest.

Coach cut her off by saying, "Listen, either you are committed or you are not. Either you want to build wealth for you and your family or you just want to squeak by and pay the bills. And you know what, Kim?"

"What?"

"If that is the highest goal you set for yourself—paying the bills—that is all you will accomplish," Coach said, sorry he had to go into a sort of "tough love" mode with her, but knowing it was necessary, "If you work until you are 65, putting away 10 percent of your earnings, guess what you will have?"

"What?" she asked, almost tearfully.

"Enough to retire, and then die at the age of 68," he said, with little mercy in his voice.

He then toned it down a bit and told her to put the pages he gave her in a notebook, like her kids did. He then asked her to go back to her suite and write down her bucket list of dreams and goals— relationships, physical goals, parenting goals, financial goals, whatever she could think of that she wanted out of life.

"Write it down," he said. "Add to it when you think of something else. This is the first step to building true wealth and making your dreams your reality."

The part about retiring at 65 and dying at 68 is what really solidified Kim's commitment. She knew she wanted a lot more out of life than just paying the bills until she died.

"Kim, you have a job with me, no matter what you decide. And as long as Mitch and Amy remain committed to their sessions with me, I will continue coaching them. But I need to know before we go further if you are truly committed."

Before Kim could answer, Coach ushered her kindly to the door, telling her they would finish the conversation the next day—about commitment to building wealth and what she needed to do next if her commitment proved true.

• • •

With the seminar completed, Coach, along with Lucy, took Jean with him so she could rest comfortably in the Gulfstream bedroom during the flight.

Prior to leaving, Coach didn't just ask Kim if she was committed to building wealth. He instead asked to see inside of her notebook. She gladly handed it over, and as he thumbed through the final few pages he found exactly what he hoped to find—a page titled, "My Vision for My Future." He didn't pry by reading each thing. He knew by the quantity of what she wrote and the fact she completed the exercise that she was indeed committed.

"Congratulations, Kim," he said, "on your new job and your newfound commitment to building wealth."

Kim and Coach agreed to meet a week later at his office in Calabasas, but only after he spent some much needed time with his family.

The twins spent two more days relaxing by the pool and playing on the beach. Mitch and Nancy had already said their sad goodbyes two days prior, promising to keep in touch.

Chapter 6

The Money House

Getting back to California felt strange for Kim and the twins. Maui had been a nice transition, but now the three were back to real life. There were still several boxes to unpack, and their new home was certainly nothing compared to the beachfront property in Malibu.

Their senior year would be starting in just over a month, and the twins decided to spend that time recharging their batteries before setting up a meeting with Coach to finally discuss and affirm their BIG reasons.

Chatting with their mom was also helpful. As an adult, she had never learned about having a goal bigger than herself and her family. However, now that she was working with Coach, she too thought daily about having a BIG reason to become wealthy, and not just to get by day-to-day.

To help ease the transition from paradise to purgatory, Kim produced two neatly wrapped gifts to her children. They were nice leather journals, and she explained how to use them to figure out their BIG reasons.

One day, while the twins were off doing other things, Kim looked around at her surroundings and sobbed. She never wanted her children to think she felt sorry for herself. Another thing she learned from Coach's seminar is that you can't spoil children by giving them money, only by giving them bad attitudes. She smiled weakly, because Mitch and Amy were taking this dramatic change in lifestyle like champs.

Kim, however, wasn't feeling so resilient. She looked around the house: the outdated linoleum floor in the kitchen and dining area, the drab grey paint she could tell used to be white from where the previous owner had hung pictures, the multi-colored brown shag carpet left over from the 1970s… She had about three months of living expenses set aside for emergencies, but she wondered how Coach would feel if she began renovating the home a little at a time. After all, she should be able to enjoy her surroundings as much as possible.

She almost grabbed her purse and keys to go to the hardware store and buy paint, look at carpeting, wallpaper, flooring, and everything it would take to turn her meager house into a home.

Just then, the phone rang. It was Coach.

"Hi Coach," she said. She looked around, wondering if he was somehow tapping into her mind telepathically, but she realized that this was just another silly coincidence.

"Kim," Coach said, "I'm calling about the job…"

Kim shuttered. He didn't decide not to hire her, did he? "I was wondering if you could start a few days early so we could use some of the time discussing your next steps."

Relieved, and yet somewhat disappointed—she really wanted to go shopping for the house—she eagerly said, "Of course, Coach. When do I start?"

Coach was also testing Kim. He threw a wrench in the program by asking her to start early, because he wanted to see how committed she was and how she would respond to a change in the game plan.

"Monday would be great," Coach said. "Oh, and Kim?"

"Yes," she said softly, looking through her calendar and feeling a little dizzy at the sudden realization that she really was starting over at square one—job, fixer-upper home, and two kids to rear on her own.

"I know in the seminar I talked about JOB meaning you are Just Over Broke. In other words, it may have sounded like a job was a bad thing. In your case of starting over, a job is paramount to your success."

Kim was a little surprised. In seminar all Coach talked about was getting past working for someone else and creating your own wealth. "Okay?" Kim said, relaying her utter confusion.

"Kim, there are steps involved in creating wealth," Coach said, "and at first, 100 percent of the income you generate is going to come from the work you do. The goal is going to be able to make enough and save enough to invest. Make sense?"

"Yes, Coach," Kim said. It did make sense. She kept hoping there would be some hidden secret in Coach's teaching—a magic bean, so to speak—that would make building wealth a painless, easy, and quick endeavor. It was starting to really sink in that she was going to have to do some hard work—and some planning and learning—before she was going to get anywhere near a fraction of Coach's level of wealth.

"Okay then, I will see you on Monday in my office. 8:30?"

"Sounds great, Coach. Thank you," she said, humbly.

"And one more thing," Coach said, as if once again reading her mind, "don't be in a hurry. Creating wealth is something you plan for—so many people fail to plan. If you fail to plan, you plan to fail. Think about it. Look at how many people spend so much time planning the wedding and zero time planning a marriage! If you want to create true wealth, you must plan it out."

"Thank you, Coach," she said. "I really appreciate your time and kindness."

She hung up the phone, looked around at her drab surroundings, and decided instead of running to the hardware store and blowing a wad of money on supplies, she would actually go to the bookstore and buy a book on home renovation.

Just like building wealth, renovating the house would take time, planning, knowledge, and work. There is no use doing something before you know what you are doing and why you are doing it.

...

It amazed Amy that the more she and her brother worked together on uncovering their individual reasons why they wanted to become wealthy, the clearer their minds became.

Then, quite suddenly, it was done. They knew exactly why they wanted to become wealthy. They sat down together and talked seriously for a moment.

"My BIG reason is to raise funds to preserve our oceans," she read from her notebook, and then turned to Mitch longingly. There is no way he could have understood how she felt about her newfound passion because he hadn't experienced it.

"I just wish you had spent some time to go diving and snorkeling with me. You'd see what I mean. Maybe I'll even be able to build aquariums people can visit so that everyone can know the beauty of the sea," Amy announced with conviction. "And what's your BIG reason?"

Unfortunately, Mitch did not quite have Amy's resolve yet–his WHY? His BIG reason for creating wealth. He looked inside the sliding glass door to the dining room to see his mother sitting on the floor, her back against the wall, deep in thought. He noticed that she seemed afraid...and then it came to him.

"My BIG reason is to be able to take care of Mom and Grandma Angie as they get on in years," Mitch said proudly.

...

Coach had been away with his family - he was back on tour, which took him and Kim to Atlanta. He was extremely happy with Kim and how well she took over Jean's position.

"Kim," Coach said as he exited his office for the day at just past one o'clock in the afternoon, "get those kids on my calendar, okay? Sometime this week."

"Sure, Coach," she said, wishing she could just come and go like he did, but still enjoying her job with him. She booked the twins for later in the week.

It seemed like forever since Amy and Mitch had seen Coach. Coach—and Lucy—welcomed them in like long lost friends.

"Hi guys, it's really great to see you two again. You are sure looking well," he beamed as he showed them into his ornate office.

They pulled up chairs and settled in for what they knew would be an interesting session.

"How have you done with your BIG reasons? Any progress?" he asked, feeling that they had finally had enough time to ruminate on them, so they could go forward with the sessions and actually begin to take actions to create wealth.

"I think we have done alright, Coach," Mitch replied. "It took us ages to come up with them, but they seem so simple now."

"That's the beauty of a well thought-out reason," Coach replied. "At the end of the day, it seems so simple. I call it a 'Blinding Flash of the Obvious,' meaning it gets to the heart of the matter, doesn't it?"

While they were talking, Amy had opened her binder and read over her BIG reason. She coughed quietly and began reading out aloud.

"My BIG reason is to raise funds to help preserve the beauty of our oceans and to build aquariums so that people, especially children, who don't have the opportunity to travel like we did, can experience sea life," she read.

"That's fantastic, Amy. That's one great and very motivating reason for wanting to grow your wealth. You are passionate about it, and I'm sure it will guide and motivate you for the rest of your life. Now what have you come up with, Mitch?"

Mitch felt his reason seemed more important on a personal level, yet wasn't nearly as far-reaching as Amy's BIG reason. "My BIG reason is to be able to take care of Mom and Grandma Angie as they get older."

"That's also a terrific reason, Mitch. Well done both of you. Can you now see how important it is to want to achieve something worthwhile? Can you understand the importance of having a well thought-out BIG reason, something that's bigger than you, bigger than just making a good living, and not just about the money and things we can buy with it?"

The twins nodded as one.

Kim, who sat at a desk right outside Coach's office, could overhear their session. She felt proud of her kids and proud of herself for rearing such good children who really took an interest in their futures.

She thumbed through the book she had purchased right before coming to work for Coach, "The Rewards of Renovation," now well-worn and dog-eared. It had become her Bible, of sorts. Fixing up the house had become something of a hobby, and she enjoyed doing with the kids on the evenings and weekends.

In one way, Kim felt contented in the moment. The kids were doing well, and the little drab house she had purchased several months ago was actually shaping up nicely. It started to feel like home to her. She finally got accustomed to being in the office eight hours a day, and it wasn't bad. With the income she made from Coach, she was able to do the very first thing she thought was her BIG reason: pay the bills, and even have a little left over to set aside.

Then it occurred to her that what she felt at that moment was exactly why Coach advised them about negative and positive BIG reasons. Indeed, she had accomplished her BIG reason, and within just a few months. The problem is, she was nowhere near wealthy. Not even close. However, she knew, thanks to Coach's lessons, that she had chosen a negative BIG reason—she focused more on what she didn't want, rather than what she wanted out of life and being wealthy.

Dreamily thumbing through her restoration book, marking projects she had completed as well as ones yet to complete, a positive BIG reason came to her. She hadn't just spent the last six months working for Coach. No, she had put blood, sweat, and tears into fixing up the house. At first, she thought it was for her own gratification and to have a nice little place to live. Now, she thought otherwise.

Kim really wanted to be a teacher like Coach. She wanted to help young women avoid the mistakes she had made, both with money and with life in general. "Planning is so important," she thought, as she was writing down her dreams and goals. Not just financial ones, but health goals, parenting goals, relationship goals...everything she wanted out of life. These had been instrumental in figuring out what she was really going for.

Kim realized then and there, at the desk outside of Coach's office, that she wanted to build wealth so that she could have more than enough money to forget working in an office job for a living, but to have a nice lifestyle that also afforded her the ability to take young women under her wing—as Coach did with Mitch and Amy—and help them build wealth of their own. She wanted young women to know that they are in charge of their own futures, and that they should never put their well being in anyone's hands but their own.

She meditated on how to make this dream, this BIG reason a reality while she stared at the pages of her book and listened to Coach instructing the twins.

"Now, I want to talk a little more about wealth, real wealth," said Coach.

He opened his folder and handed the twins a sheet of paper each.

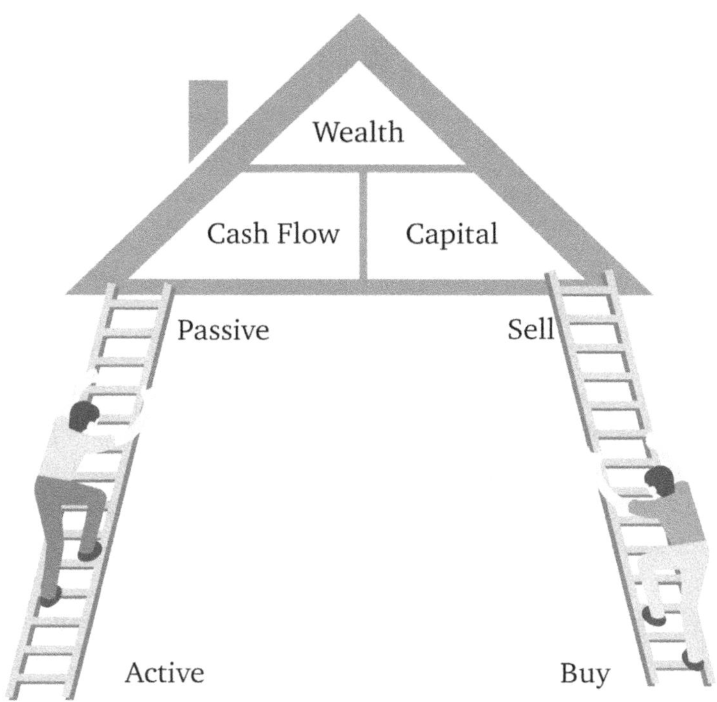

"I want you to have a good look at this diagram," Coach began. "Tell me what you feel it means to you, Amy."

"I see a roof to a house with two ladders holding the roof up from the bottom," she said. "It seems to me that it represents two paths to wealth; one has something to do with cash flow, while the other has to do with capital."

"You're definitely on the right track. Think of it this way: wealth consists of two main components—*cash flow* and *capital*," Coach explained. "Let's look at the top of the triangle first—'Wealth.'"

He opened his folder and handed them each another sheet of paper.

> **WEALTH**
> **Wealth is about more than a good income and assets. True wealth is about buying**
> **BACK MY TIME.**
> **It's about the freedom to do what I want, when I want, how I want, and with whom I want. Wealth is about building a passive income and then growing an asset portfolio.**

"Most people spend their entire lives working just to pay the bills. They maintain or slowly increase an average level of income on the one hand, and they eventually try to own a home on the other. They hope to save enough to buy a home, keep on top of the bills, and save enough to retire, but very few will ever be rich—or even well-off."

Mitch and Amy knew Coach well enough that when he spoke without asking questions, he had something extremely important to teach them. More like a professor giving a lecture, he continued. "For most people, doing great would be paying off their home, buying an investment property, and growing a small portfolio of shares in their retirement account. Very few ever even reach that. Almost none ever plan or even know how to be truly wealthy, let alone achieve it."

The twins had certainly never thought about buying homes and planning for retirement. Not at their young ages. "In fact," Kim thought, as she continued to listen in, "I haven't either."

"For some, a standard income may be fine," Coach said, now standing and gesturing wildly toward the huge grandfather clock and other opulent items in his office, "but it will never buy you back your time and freedom. It might allow you to save a few dollars to feed you during retirement, but that's about all. It's nowhere near enough to help you achieve real wealth and freedom for yourself, to achieve your BIG goals, or to facilitate early retirement."

As Mitch and Amy eagerly leaned in to learn more, Mitch finally asked the question, "So how old does someone need to be to feel comfortable retiring?"

"That's just it, Mitch," Coach said, "Always remember that retirement is not a function of age—it is a function of cash flow and capital.

"Why do *you* think an average wage and savings isn't nearly good enough, Amy?" Coach asked.

"I suppose because there is a limit to how much you can accumulate on an average salary, and you still have to go to work nearly every day to earn that salary, Coach," she replied.

Kim, listening even more intently than ever, strained to hear more. She knew she had to make some kind of leap in the next year, even a small one to facilitate generating more income than she could make on her salary alone.

"Yes, that's a big part of it," she heard Coach continue, as if he were talking to her directly, rather than the twins. "You see, if you were to rely on what you were able to generate from a salary alone, you'd limit your potential to the amount of hours you have available to work multiplied by the amount of money you make hourly. If you wanted to stop working or if for some reason you simply couldn't work, your income would, in most cases, totally stop. Then where would that leave you?"

The thought scared Kim. She imagined herself older, working on salary and getting sick or hurt, not being able to work enough to even support herself.

Coach explained further that for most adults, retirement isn't even an option. In the past, retirement used to be a milestone in nearly everyone's life. Now, he said, people literally have to keep working until they die just to pay the bills. "It's crazy," he said, "could you imagine being 50, 60, or even 70 and still *having* to work full time. And not because you wanted to either, but because you had to, just to keep paying the bills?"

Kim finally got it. This is what Coach meant when he told seminar attendees, "If all you do is set aside 10 percent of the money you earn working at a job, you will have just enough money to retire at 65 and die at 68."

Kim thought a moment. Coach was explaining the path she currently meandered down. Although she had been setting aside closer to 20 percent of her income, she realized she wasn't doing enough.

The thought of working to age 50 or even 60 didn't seem so bad, the twins thought. After all, Grandma Angie worked as a housekeeper until she was 55, but to *have to* work into your seventies? That seemed really extreme.

"Believe it or not, kiddos, most of my clients have been in that exact situation. And while everything they learn from me can help them repair their situation, just like your mom is doing, the sooner you start, the better. With most adults we have to first clean up some financial messes before we get started on the wealth building, but it all starts the same way."

Mitch leaned forward in his chair, suddenly very grateful he and Amy had gotten this beneficial jumpstart on creating wealth.

Amy reread the paper he had just given them, underlining the words with her finger, "But Coach, you say here that true wealth is about having a large *passive* income. Doesn't that conflict with what you just said?"

"Great question, Amy," Coach said, "You hit on one word that makes all the difference in this lesson."

"Which word, Coach?" a confused Mitch asked.

"It's all about developing a *passive* income." He could tell by the puzzled looks on their faces that they didn't quite understand, but he was careful not to express frustration. "Do you know what a passive income is, Mitch?" he asked.

Mitch shook his head. Amy didn't offer a reply.

"A passive income is money you receive whether you work or not. For example, income you receive from owning a successful business that you don't work in. Or royalty income like I get from the books I write, or rental income from the properties I own. It is the exact opposite of trading your time for money."

Both Mitch and Amy nodded. Now they were starting to really understand.

And so, unbeknownst to anyone in the next room, did Kim. She looked again at the book on renovation, and the answer came to her. Once she completed renovating the little home that had become a clean, modern sanctuary for herself and the twins, she was going to buy another one, move into that one, and rent out this house.

She smiled to herself, and thought, "wash, rinse, repeat. It's that simple." It is how she intended to create her own passive income and work toward creating true wealth.

Back inside Coach's office, in tune with his students and knowing by their faces that everything was sinking in, he continued. "Do either of you know roughly what a sizable asset portfolio is?"

Amy hazarded a guess, "A portfolio is a combination of someone's investment properties and shares of stock?" Amy responded.

"Yes, that's right, but it could also consist of other assets like businesses."

Coach shuffled through his folder and handed the twins another paper.

"Let's now turn our attention back to the diagram; look at the term *cash flow*."

Coach straightened up his chair, cleared his throat and took a treat from Lucy's jar. As her ears perked up, he gave it to her and continued.

"This is where nearly everyone starts. You get a job and start earning a wage. The smart ones try to save something from each paycheck so that they can begin investing or building a larger nest egg, usually with the intent of escaping the rent trap and buying their own home."

CASH FLOW

Life starts with an active income from going to work every day –

MY GOAL

is to turn my active income into a large passive income for myself over time.

Amy nodded, taking notes, as usual.

"Most, of course, never do save enough," Coach said. He walked up to the white board to the right of his desk and wrote down in large letters, "J.O.B."

"And you do know what 'J.O.B.' stands for, don't you?" he asked, not really expecting an answer.

Kim still listened from the front office. By now, she had heard this lesson so many times, she could recite it herself.

"It means 'Just Over Broke.' In reality, that's where most employees remain. They spend as much or in some cases more than they earn. My job is to help you see the futility of this and to understand how it is you can climb the cash flow ladder so you will be better off than most, even if you do nothing more and never progress beyond a large cash flow in the wealth triangle."

Mitch felt they were *finally* getting somewhere. He couldn't wait until they got down to the essence of why they were there: to create wealth. Amy, a bit more patient and savvy than her brother, knew that it was *all* important. She had to admit, though: it was getting exciting to think that they were about to be able to *do* something, and not just think about concepts. Another popular mantra of Coach's was "You earn what you learn," so they had no idea how long the learning process would be prior to actually reaping their wealthy rewards.

"What you should be trying to achieve is moving up the cash flow ladder, turning as much of your active income—that which you earn by basically trading your time and skills for money—into as much of a passive income as possible. That way you will still continue to draw an income whether you work or not."

Coach gave them the next handout.

"Don't forget that over time, your experience and

Cash flow ladder
as my experience and
knowledge grow,
I CAN MOVE
up the ladder
and watch both
my active and passive
INCOMES
grow.

knowledge base will also grow, bringing in more active income at the same time. So it's a dynamic thing that's happening here. The more active income you have, the more you can use to build your passive income base. The skill is in how you do that, and that's what we'll be working on as time goes by."

Mitch had just filed away this latest page when Coach handed them another.

"This is where most young people of your age are, including yourselves. You don't have any capital, do you?"

CAPITAL
I started with no capital at all and
MY AIM
is to build it up over time so I have a solid asset backing.

They shook their heads. With Amy's studies and Mitch's football, they didn't have time for jobs as well.

Coach waved his hand dismissively. "We all start here, but your aim must be to gradually build it up so that you end up with a solid asset base."

Mitch looked up and said, "I guess that is easier said than done, Coach."

"Only if you don't pay attention to it, Mitch. You need to keep your eye on the ball, to use sporting terminology. See, there are some simple rules to follow if you want to build up capital. The first rule is simple: *spend less than you earn*. If you remember to apply this rule, then by the time you retire you will be fairly well off. Actually, it just amounts to simple math."

"So why then do most people not stick to this simple rule, Coach?" he asked.

"They are not disciplined and they are impatient. They want 'stuff' before they can afford it. They use credit cards and end up paying a small fortune in interest."

He handed the twins a final paper for the day's session.

Capital ladder as my knowledge, **ABILITY,** and capital grow, so does my ability to **MOVE UP** the ladder and make bigger and better investment deals.

"Knowledge, ability and capital give you the capacity to do bigger and better deals. And as you will appreciate, the bigger and better the deal you do, the bigger and better the results you usually get. This is what it is all about. Move up the ladder here, and if you have moved up the cash flow ladder as well, then you will end up with great deals and a fabulous passive income. And what's more, the more time you have at your disposal, the more time you will have to chase and put together the great deals."

"So we win both ways," Mitch added, letting Coach know that he understood.

The session had been long, but it was one of the most informative yet.

They rose and made their way to the door as he spoke, very enthused, "This is where the action starts, so go and make it happen!"

• • •

They went home with their mom that evening, all pumped up and ready to go. The car ride home was invested discussing their session with their mother, who decided not to let on that she had been listening to the entire session. Mitch was first with the questions.

"So mom, how much passive income do you have right now?" he asked.

She laughed a bit, almost choking on the sip of Frappuccino she had taken. "Normally, Mitch, I would say none of your beeswax, but since I know you are learning about wealth-building, I'll tell you. I am just over the $1,000 a month mark right now, which is huge considering only a few years ago I knew nothing about how to do it. Remember, I had to pay down our debts first - credit card interest was a killer, and I really had to give up some things I had become quite used to spending a lot of money on, like clothes, makeup, and going out to eat. It's hard sometimes."

As the three drove home, Mitch noticed that they were going a bit out of the way to get there. The neighborhood was not quite as nice as the one where they currently lived, but it wasn't bad. People seemed to keep their yards up, and there weren't a lot of cars parked on the street. Suddenly, Kim pulled the car over next to a modest home that had been painted lime-green. A real estate sign with the words "FOR SALE" was planted in the ground, and their mom's smile told them there was good news on the horizon.

"What, mom?" Mitch insisted, as Kim sort of taunted them with her fixed smile.

Amy thought she had it: "You are going to buy this, aren't you?" she asked, excitedly. It was definitely a fixer-upper, with a couple dingy, dusty shutters hanging on a hinge, a burnt, overgrown lawn, very outdated curtains, and the green exterior—Amy had hoped her mother would be able to negotiate a good deal on this one.

Kim nodded with a smile.

"To rent out?" Amy asked hopefully. She really loved their current home, now that it was fully renovated.

Kim nodded again. "Eventually. But first, we are going to rent out the one we just fixed up, as soon as we finish," Kim's happiness with her decision overshadowed the twins' shock. They had just spent six months making the house perfect—and it was almost there! Now they were *moving*? To *this*?

"Mom," Mitch said, "you're crazy! We just worked our asses off—"

"Mitch!" Amy yelled, "Don't talk to mom like that!"

"Listen kids," Kim pulled them each close to listen, "I'm not going to get rich working for Coach, unless I learn while I earn. I heard his lesson today with you kids, and I know that I need to create more *passive* income in order to build wealth."

Kim explained that she learned in the seminar that getting a good deal on a home you are willing to live in for a year or so while you fix it up is brilliant. In the meantime, you work and save, and then when the house you live in is ready, buy another fixer-upper, and live in *it*, while renting the other one.

"This way," Kim recalled Coach saying, "you have an investment, 80 percent of which is being paid for by someone else. Once the loan is paid off—could be 20 years—you either have an asset that has gone way up in value, or you now get to keep *all* of the rent money as *passive* income. In the meantime, you use the equity you build along the way to keep buying new investment properties."

Though they weren't looking forward to moving again, Mitch and Amy not only thought the idea was a perfect start on their mother's road to wealth, but they were happy to see *her* putting Coach's lessons to good use.

Seeing their mother crawl out from under the rock of destitution made Mitch and Amy even more eager to put their wealth coaching to practical use in their own lives.

Chapter 7

Graduation

Kim didn't know who was more excited - her or the kids. She felt like a kid herself as she executed the final countdown of preparations for the twins' graduation party at home. It was nowhere near as extravagant as their sixteenth birthday party, but in many ways it seemed more intimate and *real*. Kim looked around. Her latest purchase, made after renting out the first home she renovated, was the one she affectionately referred to as "The Baby." She made it after purchasing her second fixer-upper, "Limey," (in reference to the home's original paint color), and it served as a tribute to Mitch and Amy's graduation. Since the kids would no longer need to be close to their school, she thought it would be fun—and ultimately lucrative—to renovate a beach house over the summer, and perhaps make it a vacation rental.

She hadn't thought of a name for this one yet. Mitch and Amy thought it silly that she felt the need to name her investment properties as if they were pets, but they *were* somewhat dear to her—in fact more dear than a pet, because pets usually don't make money! And besides, Kim thought it boring that investors referred to their properties as simply "The Jones Street property," or even just using the street name, as in referring to a home on Maple Street as "Maple."

By their third move in two years, Kim and the twins had learned to travel light. Much of their furniture stayed in storage, and only the bare essentials - beds, clothing, toiletries, minimal kitchen supplies, televisions, computers, and other basic necessities - came along on the renovation rental ride. This made "The Beach House," a two-bedroom flat-top with 1970s wood paneling and shag carpet in rust tones, a perfect party house.

For the party, with the house nearly empty, she turned the living room into a club of sorts. She let the kids invite their many friends from the private school, and she sprung for a DJ as well. One fun thing she had planned—since she was completely renovating anyway—was to let the kids paint messages on the wood-paneled walls later in the evening. She bought a bunch of sample cans of interior latex in crazy colors, some inexpensive paint brushes, and thought she would let them have at it when the time was right.

Grandma Angie had moved to Oxnard to be closer to the family, so she was there to celebrate. Also there was Jean, her husband, and their baby, Thomas, who had celebrated his first birthday several months before.

Jean had decided to not return to work for Coach. Out of loyalty to Coach she was going to return if Kim hadn't worked out, but Coach was very impressed with Kim's work, so all worked out in everyone's favor. Baby Thomas and her husband were Jean's life, and she and Kim remained close friends over the past couple of years.

Other than a few other friends and new neighbors (including Kim's latest admirers—three neighbors from her new street, whom she invited on moving day), plus around fifty of the twins' closest friends, that was the extent of the guest list.

Halfway into a dinner of pasta and salad, the doorbell rang.

Kim opened the door and clinked a spoon against her glass. "Everyone, may I have your attention. We have a special guest..."

It was Coach.

Mitch and Amy set down their plates and actually hugged Coach. "Oh, *two* special guests," Amy gushed, noticing Lucy trailing behind.

Kim had been discussing with Coach all week at the office whether she should take the twins on an overseas family vacation - their last having been the Maui trip two years prior - or give them money as a graduation gift. Coach really wanted Kim to decide on what would be the right thing to do for her family.

A vacation of their choice once they graduated seemed so appropriate. She felt that they deserved a break, and also that a vacation would serve as a line of demarcation between their teen years and adult lives.

But then she thought about the sessions and how eager the twins were to finally put Coach's wisdom to practical use. Coach's only advice was that she did what she felt in her heart. After all, her investing was starting to pay off, and what is the use of wealth if you couldn't enjoy it? He told her that there is no single path to wealth, and each of us, young or old, must choose our own way, with certain principles in mind, of course. Knowing the trip would cost nearly $10,000, he summed up his opinion with, "Whichever gift you decide, it's the same as which path to wealth you choose and when you start. No matter what, Kim, you are going to create real wealth, and so are the twins."

Coach gave a brief but powerful speech about the pride he felt for the twins, and that they were like family to him. He complimented Mitch on his decision to take the football scholarship to UCLA, and Amy for choosing to spend two years at a local college and live at home so she could save up money for her next path in life.

Were it not for his genuine interest in which gift Kim had decided to give the twins, Coach would have made a hasty exit, as he always seemed to be short on time. He was relieved when she emerged with a manila envelope addressed "To Mitch and Amy, Happy Graduation!"

The envelope contained two thin, smaller envelopes, one addressed to each twin. As they carefully tore open their envelopes in unison, their eyes widened when they pulled out checks from their mother, for $5,000 each. In just over a year working for Coach, living a much more meager existence than she had to, she was able to save enough to give her children such a generous gift, plus put down payments on her investment properties.

Others, including Coach, had given gifts of money totaling nearly an extra $2,000 each, giving them a grand total of about $7,000 a piece—more money than they had ever had to themselves, and at their own disposal as well.

Halfway through their senior year, Mitch had been awarded a full-ride scholarship to play football for UCLA. It was not too far from home, but he wanted to live in the dorms and have the full college experience. Football had always been his true passion, and although he had spent his high-school career as the Mavericks' star quarterback, he knew he wasn't likely to get to that level at UCLA. He was up against so many talented players. Like Coach—The Wealth Coach, that is—always told him, he owed it to himself and his community to give it his all.

Amy felt it would be most prudent to complete her undergraduate studies at a local community college. Then, perhaps, she would apply to UC Santa Cruz, one of the country's top schools for marine biology. It was definitely a career suited to her BIG reason for attaining wealth, but she had never heard of marine biologists being known for their wealth. She had to ponder whether she really wanted to extend her studies to marine biology, or do something that would exploit all the years of wealth education she was getting from Coach. A finance degree, perhaps?

You earn what you learn.

Just a week after graduation, Kim began encouraging the twins to pick up where they left off with Coach. She was satisfied that their lives were more stable now that they had decided on their pursuits. *Working on your wealth is not something you should start until you are ready,* Coach always taught her. *You could be ready at 18, 38, or 58. It didn't necessarily matter when you started, just as long as you did.*

...

"Hello Coach," Amy said. Her wide smile echoed the obvious joy in her heart as she and Mitch walked into the now familiarly plush office and took their seats.

"How are you two?" he asked. Not waiting for a reply, he said, "Your mother tells me you are packing up and getting ready for UCLA, Mitch. And Amy, you will be spending a couple years fulfilling the basics at community college?"

"I think so, Coach," Amy said. "To me it seems important to save the money and be close to my family."

The twins were happy when Coach approved of their decisions, even though they didn't have anything *directly* to do with pursuing wealth. In many ways, they were stepping stones to each of their BIG visions.

"So what are we going to consider today?" Coach asked rhetorically. "I think it's high time we talked about the one thing that will bring you more wealth than anything else."

Mitch looked up sharply, eager to hear what pearl of wisdom from the day's session would bring wealth faster than anything else. "Come on, Coach, give us the magic bullet!" Mitch said, excitedly as he pretended to shoot Lucy with his thumb and forefinger. Coach smiled to himself and let a moment or two pass before continuing.

"No, it's not some 'magic bullet,' Mitch. It's nothing like that at all. Like I've told you many times, there really is no trick, secret or inside knowledge to what I teach. Remember, *if it looks too good to be true, it probably is!"*

Once again, Coach handed them each a piece of paper.

"Leverage is the one concept that will do more for you than anything else. Sound too good to be true? Not at all. Even Albert Einstein referred to it when he said compound interest was one of the most amazing phenomena of the universe."

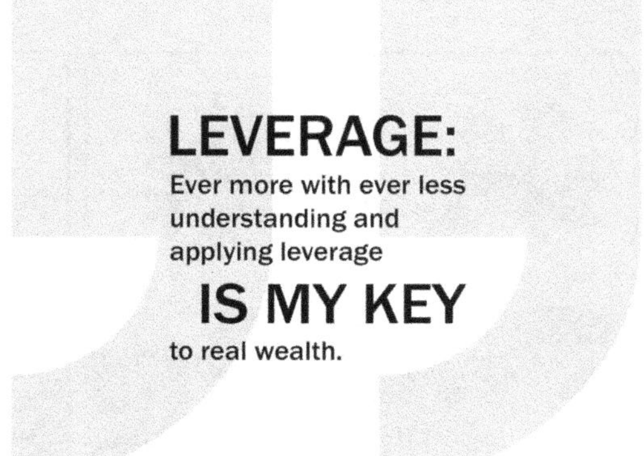

He had their full attention now.

"If you understand the concept of compound interest, you'll understand how easy it is to create wealth, but you *must* allow the time. You see, wealth takes time. It takes time to learn and time to save your starting capital. I'm assuming you have been careful with your graduation money, no?"

The twins nodded emphatically.

Coach continued. "Good - you're already ahead of the game. Wealth takes time to implement, but the most important aspect of time is that it allows investments to compound and multiply."

"When you first start out using compound interest, all the hard work takes place at the beginning of the process, and it feels like nothing is happening. You must have patience at this time, just like your mom has been doing with her property investments."

Once again, Kim could overhear Coach from her desk. *Nothing happening?* she thought. She supposed if purchasing, renovating, and renting out three homes in two years was nothing, then nothing *was* happening. No, she knew what Coach meant, and wasn't angry or even offended. She wondered if maybe she was just a little disappointed that by the time all of this work came to fruition—by becoming passive income—she would be in her sixties. She then thought about her mother, and how she, well into her sixties, had a great lust for life and had plenty of fun, all without the benefit of wealth. Kim could only imagine what Angie would do if she had created a wealthy lifestyle for herself.

She listened in again, intently, as Coach went on:

Kim smiled, reassured that her hard work—and patience—would pay off in the long run. With the beach house, she had to restrain herself from doing everything she had wanted to make it perfect. The home truly needed a complete remodel, not just a renovation.

However, Kim had done what she could. She made relatively inexpensive, yet aesthetically pleasing changes that really made a difference in the prices she could charge whether she decided to make it a vacation home or a regular rental. She would need to discuss this with Coach.

Back in the "classroom," Mitch had to use another football analogy to prove to Coach that he got the concept of leverage. "When you first start learning to play, you have to work very hard at the basics. You don't think much about strategy or game craft, but when you get more experienced, that all just falls into place. It happens without having to think about it."

"Exactly," Coach said. "So where does the leverage come in in that example, Mitch?" he asked. "I mean, what is being leveraged?"

"I suppose the player is leveraging his ... experience, Coach?"

"That's right, Mitch. That's exactly right."

Coach knew that Mitch instinctively knew the answer. He simply needed to draw it out of him. "After all," Coach thought, "this is the essence of coaching."

"Now, let's put all of this into monetary terms. Imagine starting on your path to wealth by investing just one cent," Coach continued. "That's right, one cent. Let's assume that this small investmet was to double in value each and every day until the last day of the month."

He paused so that Amy could catch up with her note-taking.

"Now remember what I said about the hard work taking place up front before critical mass kicks in? In this hypothetical scenario, this is what your investment would look like as it grew." He walked over to the white board again, and began writing furiously:

Day 1: 1¢	Day 4: 8¢
Day 2: 2¢	Day 5: 16¢
Day 3: 4¢	Day 6: 32¢

Coach stopped to give his hand a break, "I leave it to you to work out the rest, but let me ask you this before you do. What do you think that single cent would have grown to in value by day 15, or half way through the month?"

Amy quickly began scribbling numbers down the side of her page while Mitch noisily went through the motions of doing mental arithmetic. Neither of the twins arrived at an answer.

Coach picked up his dry-erase marker again and wrote as he spoke. "It would only be worth $163.84."

"Day 15: $163.84"

"OK, here's the interesting part," Coach said, "What do you think it would be worth on day 31?"

Again Amy's pencil jerked into life and Mitch scratched is head.

"Would you believe..." and Coach wrote on the board:

"Day 31: $10,737,418.24!!!"

"Over ten million dollars!?" exclaimed Mitch in utter amazement.

"This is a very graphic—and unlikely—illustration of the compounding effect," Coach said, happy that its impact was not lost on his students.

Now that the twins understood the idea of compounding interest, it was time for another sheet. He carefully flipped open his folder, extracted two sheets, and handed them out.

Input to output
at the start
my effort and input
ARE HIGH,
but when I work it right,
my output
– OR RESULT –
grows, and my input
decreases over time.

"When you put the concept of leverage into a wealth creation concept, what it means is that you need to work hard creating and growing your wealth in the beginning," Coach explained, "and then as time goes by, the amount of energy and effort diminishes and the returns on your energy and effort grow."

Amy wrote furiously as Coach continued, "Think of it like a see-saw. In the beginning, your effort and amount of work you put in is high, while the result, or output, is low. Then, as time passes and the results of your input and effort add up, the results or output start to mount until a point is reached where the two are balanced."

Coach stood, animatedly miming this concept, now with his arms outstretched, left arm up and right arm down like a see-saw.

"Think of my left arm as your effort and workload, and my right arm as results and output."

As he spoke, he moved his arms so that they were both balanced. He paused there for a moment so that the twins could see the effect of his explanation. As he continued speaking, he slowly continued moving his arms until the left one was at the lowest point and the right one was up high.

"Now can you see what is happening? My left arm, which represents my effort and work, is right down low, meaning you are not putting in as much as before, while my right arm, which equals results, is sky high."

Amy nodded as she finished sketching the see-saw analogy in her note pad.

"That's what's happening now with us, isn't it, Coach?" Mitch asked. "We are putting in the hours and effort learning how to go about creating wealth, but in years to come, the amount of time needed for learning will get less, but the results of what we are doing will increase."

Mitch had grasped the concept well. "The ultimate point is," Coach said, "if you do it right, at first you *make* money. Then as you invest more and more, you graduate to a point where your time is invested in *managing* money."

He then knelt on one knee and looked the twins squarely in the eyes. "Understand that this concept works on the idea that what you invest in the early days determines what you will reap later on, so remember this:" He handed each of the twins a third sheet of paper.

Divide to multiply
the mathematic formula
for leverage
HELPS ME
understand
that for growth,
I HAVE
to divide
so that I can multiply.

Just when they thought they had grasped everything so well, they were absolutely confused.

"It's not that long ago when we were at school, Coach, but for the life of me, I can't seem to recall how it is you multiply by dividing," Mitch said. "Surely to multiply you need to multiply?"

Coach always enjoyed discussing this one, as it got everyone thinking. Most people struggled to grasp the concept here and seldom understood it without his having to explain it carefully. This time was no different.

"Think of it this way, if you multiply one by itself, all you get is one. There are many examples of dividing to multiply in life and in business. Think of the Henry Ford Production line. It's a perfect example. Can either of you tell me how?" Coach asked.

"Who?" the twins asked, each completely perplexed.

As Kim continued to listen from her desk, she couldn't help but snicker out loud. Had Coach lost it? They wouldn't know who Henry Ford was. She only knew a little about him from history class many moons prior, but she thought it cute, and continued to listen.

Both students stared blankly and tried to remember—who was Henry Ford?

Coach briefly explained that in 1913, Henry Ford installed the first moving assembly line for the mass production of an entire automobile. His innovation reduced the time it took to build a car from more than 12 hours to two hours and 30 minutes.

The twins wanted to know more, but they knew Coach's time was valuable. Plus, they could Google that.

Coach just figured that the twins, like most students, would take some time and further explanation to understand the concept of leverage.

"If you think about it as I've just described it, you will see that it is still rather simplistic. You could do a lot better by pushing the concept further. Use even more leverage, if you like, by not relying on just one main piece of effort or input, but rather lots of little pieces of effort or input. This way the principle works even more efficiently because lots of different inputs produce multiple outputs."

"Ah, so by dividing your inputs, you multiply your outputs," said Mitch in amazement. "You divide to multiply."

"Exactly," responded Coach, clearly delighted his young student had grasped the gist of the concept.

"But that's not the end of this thing called leverage," Coach continued. Amy looked clearly surprised. She couldn't imagine what there could be still that could work for them that they hadn't already gone over.

"Amazing, isn't it?" Coach continued and handed them another sheet of paper.

"Oh, now I get it Coach!" Amy said excitedly. "It's absolutely brilliant, like what you explained in our last session."

"Right, Amy. Think of someone who writes a book. How many times do they write the book?"

"Once, Coach," she replied.

"And how many times can they sell the book? I mean, how many times can they get paid from selling the book, never mind revisions and new editions?"

Get paid forever
leverage for me is about doing
MY WORK
once and getting paid for it
LONG-TERM
or hopefully forever.

"That depends on how many books they sell," she responded.

"Exactly, Amy. The author writes the book once and, ideally, gets paid for it forever through what are called 'royalties.' And it's not just authors, but musicians, or filmmakers, or..."

"What about business owners?" Mitch asked.

"Great thinking, Mitch." Coach was clearly impressed.

Coach was excited that they were getting the point. Leverage is all about long-term results.

Kim knew that the kids really understood Coach's lessons, but she also knew that she had lived his lessons—in the past and now. It used to be that she worked once and got paid once, like the average person—and much like she did now with her day job, working for Coach.

However, she liked to think of her job with Coach as a transitional phase where she had created enough income to be able to keep investing. She was actively doing that, earning passive income on the two rentals she had already put the work into. She wasn't reaping the rewards yet, but she was able to collect enough rent to pay for almost her entire investment. She knew that if she kept going in this direction, one day it would all come back to her, and then some.

As the session began drawing to a close, Coach handed the twins one more sheet of paper for their notebooks.

"This is another aspect of the concept of leverage," Coach said, "This is something else that enables leverage to produce spectacular results in the long term."

> Compounding
> – time and rate –
> leverage uses the effect of compounding.
> **THE HIGHER**
> the percentage rate and the longer the time,
> **THE BETTER**
> the leverage.

Mitch and Amy, along with their benignly eavesdropping mother, were becoming truly cognizant of financial matters and had now begun to automatically think from a financial viewpoint.

"I have some homework for you to do before our next session."

Mitch looked up in surprise. Coach hadn't given them homework for some time.

"I want you to go home now and think hard about compounding" Coach said, noticing Mitch and Amy's eager expressions becoming a little stale. Even though they understood Coach had good reasons, they were tired of their homework only being about *thinking*. They wanted to *do*.

Coach readily picked up on their disappointment. Well, to put it like Elvis, they wanted a little less conversation and a little more action. He smiled and rubbed his hands together, letting the moment of suspense linger a bit. "...And when you've done that, I want you to do this: find yourselves an investment that will give you the best return based on the two elements of compounding you learned today—time and rate. Then, when you have found the investment that you believe offers the best return, I want you to start your investment portfolio off by actually investing some of that graduation money. Is that clear?"

"You mean you want us to find a real investment to put our money in, Coach?" Mitch asked with a twinge of nervousness in his voice.

"That's right, Mitch. You really need to dip your toe in the water sooner or later, and there's no time like the present...no pun intended. You see, this is what I have been telling you all along—the sooner you start, the better because of the time factor. Find an investment, and run it by me before you act on it."

The twins left, knowing that their learning was just beginning.

Chapter 8

COLLEGE

The summer of their 18th year was the first time the twins had ever been separated long-term. Amy was glad that she had decided to stay home and go to community college. She and Kim made it a mother-daughter thing to buy and fix up the investment homes, and now they were ready to make another move. Amy found one closer to UCLA, now that the beach house was ready to be rented. Though the home was further from her school, Kim could get it at an auction for a pittance compared to going through a realtor.

Mitch had to leave for UCLA a month earlier than the other students for football training. He took his uniform bag and headed down the stairwell at Kerkoff Hall, where they housed many of the fall athletes. He couldn't help but notice two giggling cheerleaders in front of him wearing skimpy blue and white Bruins outfits, one with long black hair that reminded him of...wait...could it be?

He jogged down the steps faster to get a closer look. "Nancy?" he, put down his uniform bag.

Even lovelier than ever, she turned around, smiled brightly and hugged him tight around the neck. "Mitch! I thought I'd never see you again!"

"So," Kim asked Amy on the way to the new fixer-upper, after dropping Mitch at school, "what is next on the agenda with Coach?"

"Well mom, Coach told us to find an investment opportunity that would give us great results based on time and rate. I know you already know the concept, but you know what I found?"

Kim shook her head in glowing anticipation. The entire family was hooked on building wealth.

"I visited the bank and asked them about investment options. I said I wanted to invest $1,000," Amy said, feeling so grown-up talking about investing money with her mother. "The banker asked me for how long I wanted to invest the money. I said either six months or a year."

For a moment, Kim was glad Amy only wanted to invest $1,000. Even though she was doing well—with her job and her properties—she couldn't necessarily rescue either of the twins financially, come what may. Besides, pursuant to her BIG reason, she wanted her daughter to be independent, *especially* financially.

"For a six month term my investment would grow by 4.35 percent, but if I left it in for a year, it would grow by 4.55 percent. That shows quite well what Coach was talking about, doesn't it? *The longer the time, the greater the rate.* But then I asked, just to sound like I was serious and not wasting their time, what the rates would be if I were to invest $5,000."

"And how did that turn out?" Kim asked, her head buzzing. She wished Amy would go in on a down payment for a home with her, but that wasn't the assignment. Kim knew Coach wanted the twins to learn about the time and interest concept.

"I could get 5.15 percent for six months and 5.30 percent for a year."

"So what have you decided?"

"I almost deposited the entire $5,000 immediately, but I have to run it by Coach first," Amy said, a little deflated.

"Good girl," Kim said, relieved. "Remember, this whole process is about learning and patience."

...

After practice, Mitch and Nancy stayed up all night sitting on the stadium steps, catching up. At first she said that her feelings were a little hurt because he didn't keep in touch. "What about *you*?!" he retorted.

"I didn't want you to think I was some weird stalker chick or something," she said, snuggling up a little closer. Mitch smiled to himself. He was cautiously optimistic that fate had just handed him a trump card... but he didn't want to get carried away. Besides, he thought it best that they get to know each other all over again, as well as make sure that they were still compatible after two years and without the romantic surroundings of Hawaii.

The shrill ring of the telephone woke him up way too early the next morning. It was Amy. After an obnoxiously loud yawn right into the receiver, he woke up a little and remembered to tell Amy about running into Nancy again after so long.

"Well," she said, genuinely happy for him, "I have an announcement as well."

"Okay?" Mitch yawned.

"I am going to invest—as long as Coach approves it—my $5,000 in savings. In just one year I will earn 5.3 percent interest."

"That's super, Amy!" Mitch told her, not knowing quite how to tell her that Coach would not approve- he'd already tried it. When he phoned his mother at work a few days before, Coach had just come into the office.

"Mitch," Kim had said, as Coach walked by her desk, "Coach is back from his trip..."

"Oh, nice. Tell him hi for me, mom."

"Mitch McConnell!" Kim had run out of patience with Mitch not remembering he had homework elsewhere besides school. "Coach... homework?"

Mitch had laughed at his mother for not knowing he was already a step ahead of her and had done his research. "Mom, do me a favor and put Coach on the phone."

It was then that Coach told him that putting his money into an interest-bearing account and letting it mature indeed was an example of time and rate compounding. “But,” Coach asked him in a way Mitch already knew was the answer, “is it the *best* option?”

Coach had advised Mitch to go do a little more research and get back to him.

As Mitch told the story, Amy felt relieved she hadn’t acted impulsively and deposited the money. It never would have occurred to her that her brother would beat her to the punch though. She listened intently to his experience.

After talking to Coach, he had gone back and told the bank that he had $1,000 to invest and wanted to get the best return, taking into account rate and time. “In the first of two scenarios,” he said, “I invest $1,000 for two years at 5 percent interest. This would return me $1,105. But if I were to add an additional $100 every month for the term of the investment, I would have $3,634 to show at the end of the two year period.”

Amy was clearly impressed with her brother. Mitch had packed his things, moved to a new town, started football, gotten a girlfriend *and* did his homework too—all in just a few days time.

“So what is the second scenario?” she asked.

“Scenario two: Here I would again start with $1,000, but this time I would leave it in for four years. If I were to invest nothing further, then at the end of the term, my investment would be worth $1,221. *But* if I were to increase my investment by $100 a month over the four years, guess what I would receive at the end?”

“Tell me,” Amy said.

“$6,544. Isn’t that something?” Mitch replied. “So I’ve settled on this option, and Coach thinks it’s good. I figured that I’d add a little part-time job on the side for extra money to make my investment and do stuff with Nancy.”

“So you did exactly what Coach wanted you to do—play with the two variables of rate and time,” she noticed. “And while the actual percentage rate may remain static, I think by increasing the amount invested you will be increasing the rate of return on the money you are investing. Plus, you chose a longer time span to benefit from that factor as well. But Mitch, why not invest all $3,000 you have saved?"

"I'm not sure. I might invest more, but you never know when you are going to need immediate cash." He was glad that Amy got exactly what he was doing, though he did feel that he should invest more than $1,000 as well. He didn't know how he was going to pull off going to school, playing football, having a girlfriend, *and* getting a part-time job all at once. Well, Coach did say that the initial input would be high!

• • •

The next day was Sunday. "No practice," Mitch thought thankfully as he dismissed his seven o'clock alarm and rolled over to go back to sleep. He tossed and turned, but the blinding light that peeked through the curtains did him no good.

He decided to give up on sleep and take a morning run around his new collegiate neighborhood. He passed at least fifteen coffee bars, bookstores (new and used), juice bars, quaint cafés, bars, and other little specialty shops. Most stores were still closed, but the coffee and juice bars were open.

After his run, Mitch grabbed a shot of espresso and a small cup of wheatgrass juice. As he strolled back to the dorm down a side street, to his surprise he found a shop open already at eight o'clock in the morning. "Cool," he thought, when he noticed it was a sporting goods store.

An older man swept the front steps whistling a tune and shaking his head at the neon sign that, due to a missing light bulb, read "**an us sporting goods.**" It was supposed to be "**angus sporting goods**," which wasn't so bad in the daylight, but he would have to take care of it before nightfall or risk being a laughing stock.

"Good day, lad," the man said with a thick Irish accent.

"Good morning, Sir. How are you?" Mitch replied.

"Well, I'd be better if me sign didn't say '**anus**,'" and he chuckled heartily, pointing to the sign.

Mitch laughed so hard he almost spit out his juice, but he restrained himself. The man shook his head and grumbled a bit. "Yeah, me wife used to take care of all this crap, but now all she wants to do is tend to her garden and spend time with the grandkids."

The man was quite animated and amusing, waving his hands around and laughing at his own dilemmas, then cursing them right afterward. Mitch looked past the man, past the bright blue open glass door, and into the store itself. It was certainly no Dick's Sporting Goods, but there was something interesting about it. Then, all of a sudden, it came to him.

"Sir, my name is Mitch McConnell," he extended his hand. The man, seemingly impressed, put the broom aside and met Mitch's firm, but gentle handshake.

"What is this 'Sir' business?" the man said, mock-scolding Mitch, "The name is Paddy Ryan."

"Kind of a neat store you have, Mr. Ryan," Mitch said carefully. "I am pretty busy—I'm starting as a freshman redshirt, but I still have practice almost every day. Then classes start in a month, but I have a proposal for you, Mr. Ryan."

"Oh, I thought a strapping young lad like yourself you might be on the Bruins. And for goodness sake, call me Paddy. Mr. Ryan was me father."

"Ok, Paddy," Mitch said confidently, "Pardon me for being blunt, but it really looks like you could use some help around here."

Paddy shook his head, "That I could, lad. That I could. But I can't afford paid help. Ahhhh, and me wife. I love her to pieces, but she won't help out anymore. I'm telling you, these women..."

Mitch politely cut Paddy off to get to his point, "Well, Paddy, it looks to me like you can't afford *not* to have help. And I could use a flexible part-time job. I'd be willing to take a little less in pay for the flexibility."

Paddy, now staring Mitch down, was definitely impressed. The boy was certainly an athlete, and well-mannered. Mitch met Paddy's eye contact and held it there. "Okay," Paddy said, pointing a finger, "But I ain't paying you a penny over ten dollars an hour. And if I catch you stealin' from me I'll cut off yer hand."

Mitch laughed to himself. "Yessir. I mean no, Sir. I mean..."

"Just spit it out, lad!" Paddy said semi-impatiently.

"Thanks, Paddy," he said, finally. He would have easily settled for eight dollars an hour, but he was beginning to know the game. "And I was hoping for eleven dollars an hour, but ten works for me. I'll be back in a bit to fix the sign, and anything else you need."

Patty, just waved him off, in mock disgust, but looked up at the last minute and winked at his new employee...his first ever.

He and Paddy would become good buddies, Mitch could tell.

• • •

For Amy, things were not faring so well. A junior college really wasn't challenging enough for her. With her intellect, she really could have had her pick of the litter as far as schools went. She just sort of lost interest in school when the financial devastation following Bryce's death hit the family. Truly, the financial crisis that pried Amy's interest from her own future and her own dreams had led her to a decision that may have been a negative decision.

Now that her mother was well on her way to bailing her out of the financial mess and swimming toward wealthier shores, she no longer felt that need to cling to home.

Then again, how would they pay for a good college? She wasn't academic scholarship material, though she figured she could have gotten grants or even loans. However, she had heard horror stories about college kids selling out their futures by taking out student loans.

Amy decided it was time to make some changes in her own life, to propel her future in the direction she wanted it to go in. As she loaded the dishwasher she looked over at her mother sitting at the dining table, perusing some real estate magazines and several newspapers. They included properties from Bakersfield to San Diego, from Nevada to Oregon. Her mother, she thought, seemed content. She was really into the real estate thing and still loved her job with Coach.

Kim looked up from her reading. "What is it, baby?"

"What's what?" Amy asked.

Kim gave her daughter "the look" that said, "Come on, spit it out. I know there is something on your mind." She patted the chair next to her, indicating that Amy come sit down and talk it out.

"Mom," Amy said, carefully, "you know I love living with you and being close to Grandma, but I always thought that I would do more academically. I'm really not happy at the junior college, and I just don't know what to do. I know I have a promising future. Coach has taught me so much. I just feel like I'm not putting it to full use staying here."

Kim looked at her with downturned eyes. Amy, afraid that she had hurt her mother's feelings, said, "But mom, I'm not going to move. I'm just going to finish college here, and we'll see what's next."

Kim put a finger to Amy's lips, "Now you shush, little girl. First of all, you are a smart, kind, and beautiful young lady. You've spent all this time with Coach. What do you think he would say?"

Amy thought for a moment. "That I'm not pursuing wealth in a way that will ultimately fulfill my BIG reason? That I'm not pursuing my dreams?"

Kim nodded knowingly. "Look Amy, I love you. You are welcome to live here with me whenever you want. I love it. But I also understand that you have your own life, your own dreams." She paused for a moment, taking Amy's hand with both of hers. "You know what I think?"

"What mom?" Amy asked.

"I think it's time for us to schedule another session with Coach."

• • •

Amy, perturbed that Mitch was *so busy* he couldn't bother to come see Coach for two weeks, didn't wait in the lobby for her brother as she usually did. She just went right on up. Coach didn't exactly sit around in his office. In fact, he only came in very rarely. He usually spent time teaching seminars about wealth to massive groups around the world, writing his books, or reaping the rewards of all his earlier hard work and traveling with family. When Mitch did decide to grace everyone with his presence, it had to be a Sunday because it was the only day he had neither practice nor class. Amy laughed aloud at her own double entendre—*Mitch has no class*.

Interestingly enough, when she let herself into the office and knocked on Coach's door, it was Mitch's voice that said, "Come in."

Mitch read to himself a piece of paper, the next one for their notebook. One lay in front of Amy's place at the desk. "Hi," she said, somewhat coldly.

"Hello," Mitch said in an equally curt manner.

"Where's Coach?" Amy asked.

"Uh, I think he had to take Lucy out. I really don't know."

"What's with the attitude?" she said. Before Mitch could answer, Coach cleared his throat to announce his presence.

"Go ahead Amy, get caught up with your brother," Coach said, seeming concerned.

Slightly embarrassed, Amy silently read her paper. She knew she was being hypocritical - and perhaps a little jealous at the fact that Mitch had so much going on in his life, yet he still had time for the sessions with Coach.

Coach allowed his young students to digest what they had just read before speaking.

> Critical mass compounding and leverage bring me to a point of growth known as **"CRITICAL MASS"**, where I have already done all the work and the results just keep **GROWING** and self-perpetuating.

Mitch read it, but he had to tell Amy and Coach about Paddy, Angus Sporting Goods, and how it would help him earn the money to increase his investment.

"Good God, son," Coach said. "Football, classes, a girl, and a job now too?"

Amy held back tears. "I just feel like my BIG reason, my BIG vision, is getting lost going to that small school that doesn't challenge me whatsoever. I have no social life, and I guess...well...I'm a little envious of Mitch and his new life."

Coach gave Amy an approving look, like he appreciated her honesty and also that she had recognized she felt she was losing her way, her dream, her BIG reason. "Amy, Mitch, I am equally proud of both of you. Remember our first lessons about decisions and reasons for choosing wealth? You are both using those lessons to evaluate your lives right now. Amy, I can't tell you what to do to change your circumstances, but I can tell you that I have faith that you will do the right things to get back on track."

And with those words, the session continued.

"Before we discuss how you did with the assignment I gave you, I'd like to delve a little deeper into the concept of leverage for a moment," he began.

"I'm sure you now see the benefits of rate and time as far as results are concerned."

They nodded vigorously.

"Now think about what the results will be if you had many investments, all working away simultaneously for you. What result do you think you would achieve? Think of it in terms of your experience gained as a result of your assignment."

Amy was first to speak. "If I had a range of investments, some with longer terms and higher rates and others with shorter terms and lower rates, then I would probably be reaping a nice steady income, wouldn't I?"

"And we would have a portfolio that would be growing on its own," Mitch added.

Impressed, Coach reinforced his point. "That's right. You would reach the point of *critical mass*, which is the stage at which your investment would be self-perpetuating. It would be able to provide you a good return while also growing on its own the entire time. You would then need very little input while receiving a terrific output."

Amy completed her notes and then paused, expecting Coach to continue. Instead, he began inquiring about their first foray into the investment market.

Mitch then outlined what he and Coach had discussed. He really wanted to invest just $1,000 for the time being, adding to his investment monthly with the income he made working at the sporting goods store. He liked this choice because momentum was built into it.

Amy reluctantly admitted that she had wanted to invest all $5,000 in a low-interest bearing savings account. Mitch told him her idea (which he never disclosed was Coach's idea all along), but that now she wanted to do what Mitch had done, using all the money. She, too, wanted to work, and reap the rewards of passive income down the line.

Coach reached for his manila folder, selected another sheet and passed it around.

"Now do you both understand why your original plan had no built-in momentum?" Coach asked.

Amy spoke the obvious, "I don't have any income like Mitch does."

> Momentum
> I need to remember that to get wealth growing or a train moving, takes massive
> **EFFORT**
> at the start, but once it's running, I just need to tend
> **THE FIRES.**

"The point I want to make is this: at first, Mitch will likely find it tough adding to his investment by an additional $100 every month. But I'd say that by year three he probably won't even notice it, since he will be so used to paying it," Coach said.

They continued to discuss the merits of Mitch's choice to work and go to school, to add to his investment, and whether Amy really wanted to follow suit.

• • •

The tumultuous days following the twins' coaching session wore on both Kim and the twins. They had taken in so much during the session and now had the time to reflect upon what it all meant—how it applied to, or affected, their investment decisions going forward.

Mitch was more than just excited, while Amy found that she was slightly disappointed in herself; she felt constrained by her current rut. The more they talked about it, the more she found herself eager to find a way to do better. She particularly liked the notions of critical mass and momentum; she wanted to make sure that whatever she did, it would include them from now on.

"I've got to find a way to afford an investment just like the one you have, Mitch," she said. "I mean, I am going to invest the $1,000, but I'm going to need to work too in order to give it the same momentum as your investment," Amy sunk back into the sofa at their mother's latest fixer-upper and looked forlornly at her brother. He was lucky to have a flexible, yet steady job and an income, she thought. She knew now that if he could handle all the things on this plate, she should get busy making some money so she could invest more.

"I really think you have done okay, Amy," Kim said, after overhearing enough of Amy's woeful attitude. She sat down in between her two children. "We've really been through a lot in the last couple of years, and you have been there for me, Amy. You stayed at community college to save money when you were smart enough to go to Stanford. After dinner, let's really think about how you are going to improve your life, financially and otherwise."

"Okay, mom," Amy said hopefully, wondering what creative solution her mother would ultimately suggest.

"I made your favorite, Mitch," Kim said enticingly. "Meatloaf and mashed potatoes."

He couldn't wait. A home-cooked meal after all that dorm food sounded heavenly.

Amy couldn't have cared less about the food. She ate like a bird anyway, and she ate her mom's cooking nearly every night, so it wasn't a big deal. The big deal was these next steps Amy was going to take.

The doorbell rang. It was Grandma Angie, joining the family for dinner. As everyone filled their plates, Kim decided to begin the conversation regarding what she and Amy had discussed days prior—about her wanting to leave the nest. She was only one semester into college, the same as Mitch. She would attend one more semester at home, apply to a college that suited her, and get back on track with her BIG reason. Plus, she needed to start working and saving money.

Grandma Angie pouted, "How far away are you going, dear?"

"Grandma, like mom said, I'll finish out the upcoming semester at my current school, continue to help Mom with the rentals, be here for summer, and then who knows? I'll probably stay in California. I *really* want to transfer to UC Santa Cruz. Their marine biology program is one of the best in the world!"

They all talked away the rest of the dinner. Amy was even more talkative than usual, and her mother immediately knew that positive decisions were on the horizon. She loved it when her children became passionate about something, and seeing the passion return in Amy's demeanor, her face even seeming brighter, delighted Kim.

"And Mitch, how are things going at the sporting goods store?" Grandma Angie asked, her eyes not really focused on him. "Is Paddy still a hoot?"

The family had gone to UCLA a few months prior to see Mitch, go to a game, see the famous Angus Sporting Goods, and last, but certainly not least, meet Nancy, who Mitch had been going steady with for nearly six months. Everyone most definitely approved.

"He is a crack-up, grandma," Mitch said, trying to remain positive. "I just...I'm a little worried about him. It's like he's aged a lot over the last six months. He stopped making fat jokes about his wife, and he's moodier than before. It's like there is something going on, but I'm not sure what it is."

"Well," Kim seemed a little worried, "how are sales doing? The business seemed to be booming when we were there."

"That's the thing," Mitch said, taking center stage since it seemed everyone agreed that Amy needed to make some changes, "I've gotten more involved in ordering inventory and selling the products. I found a new kind of shirt and underwear made out of this material they just invented that wicks the sweat away better than anything they've ever made..."

"Gross!" Amy said. "Really, during dinner?"

Mitch, flushed with enthusiasm, did not care. "We have an exclusive contract, thanks to yours truly, to sell the garments, so our sales have jumped dramatically. I just keep researching the newest and best of everything and try to get it into the store. Anything outdated goes on clearance. Plus, I've told all my friends, and they buy everything from Paddy."

"So why isn't he happy? The store is doing well." Kim asked.

"Yeah, I haven't seen the books or anything, but he told me one day when he was in a good mood that thanks to me, his revenue was twice what it had been the same time last year. And because it's steady, he's raised me to

$15 per hour, plus commission," Mitch reasoned, "but I don't know. Some days he's all bright and smiley, and some days he's either down in the dumps or doesn't come in at all while I'm there."

"Hmmmm," Grandma Angie speculated, "Paddy is about my age. Maybe he is just getting old and tired. I'm sure he appreciates having you."

"Yeah, he does," Mitch continued, "and now that I'm able to add even more to my investment, I want to meet with Coach again soon. We didn't have enough time at today's session to bring it up, but I even have a little extra set aside for another investment." He hadn't wanted to brag about it in front of Amy, but she would be alright. Plus, maybe a little competition would get her off of her backside and get working.

Amy began clearing the plates. She wasn't the least bit upset. She had a plan, and was eager to execute it. She felt that feeling people get when they just know life is going to change for the better.

Angie yawned and looked at the large wall clock, but couldn't make out the time regardless of the abnormally big numbers. "Well kids," she said, giving everyone a big hug and kiss on the cheek, "I'm gonna get my tired old butt home and to bed."

Kim hugged her mother and said, "You get some rest."

"Bye grandma!" the twins said. They walked her to the door, and then Mitch walked her all the way to her car, parked in the driveway.

As he returned to help clean up dinner, they heard a loud thud. They all looked out the kitchen window.

"Oh shit!" Mitch exclaimed, "grandma hit my jeep."

"Is she okay?" Amy panicked as they all ran outside.

She was alright, just a little shaken. "That jeep just came out of nowhere," she complained, embarrassed.

"Mom," Kim said, "come back inside. Let's make sure you are okay."

"I am absolutely fine!" Angie snapped. "Mitch, honey, I'm sorry. You get me the estimates on fixing that bumper, and we'll get it fixed. Luckily, my deductible is only $500."

The twins thought, "*Only*?"

Kim asked Amy to drive Grandma home in her car, and she would follow in hers to bring Amy back. After a little grumbling from Angie, she got out of the car and Amy took the driver's seat.

Kim put her hand to her forehead as the two took off. "Honey, I'm so sorry," she said to Mitch as he squatted to assess the damage.

"Ah, don't worry about it mom. I'm just glad grandma's okay," he said, his arm around her.

"You've grown into such a good man," Kim said sentimentally. "Well, honey, you better get on the road now. It's getting late, and you've got a big day tomorrow. And seriously, get those estimates, and grandma will pay to have that bumper fixed."

Kim pulled out of the garage to retrieve Amy from Angie's house. She was afraid it was time to have *the talk* all elderly drivers despise. She would take her to get her eyes looked at, but it was probably time for Angie to relinquish driving. With her job and investment income, Kim could afford to hire a driver for her mom a few hours a week

"I don't want some stranger carting me around," Angie said stubbornly.

Amy immediately realized that if her mother could pay someone else to drive her grandma, she certainly could pay her own daughter.

"What if I do it, grandma?"

Kim, surprised by her daughter's eagerness to jump in and help, stood back to see what this was all about.

Angie, always a sucker to spend time with her grandchildren, instantly perked up and said, "Well, now, there's an idea!" She shot Kim a look. "Driver! Hmmmph!"

"Okay, mom," Kim said, "I guess you have a new driver. And Amy, you have a new job."

* * *

Kim had much to do in order to prepare for the next seminar, which was just six weeks away and in Boston. Coach rarely came into the office, but she could always get in touch with him if she needed. She had almost forgotten to look at his calendar between now and then to get the twins in for another session.

As it so happened, he was available in two weeks. "Coach, thank you so much for staying with Mitch and Amy over the years," Kim said when she spoke with him on the phone.

"You know, Kim," Coach said quite seriously, "It has truly been—is truly—a pleasure. When Mitch and Amy saved Lucy's life back in Maui, I really felt I had to give back something of value, but I wanted to make sure my knowledge was something they would take to. They certainly have, so I can honestly say it is my pleasure. It also isn't over yet. We still have much work to do."

In the meantime, Amy went to her school counselor and advised him of her plans to transfer after the next semester. He looked at her transcripts and said, "We'll sure be sorry to see you go so soon, Amy, but I can certainly see how someone with your grades and aptitudes would want to move on to her true passion."

He then gave her the good news that with Cal Grants and Pell Grants, plus a few academic scholarships for which he advised her to apply, he believed her entire education, including most living expenses would be subsidized. That was a huge relief.

The next, more difficult step, was being accepted at the school of her choice. She noticed the hefty application fees, and internally balked. But before she could say anything, her counselor suggested that she choose three colleges: one she was sure she could get into, one she had a reasonably good chance of getting into, and one "dream school" that she had a chance for acceptance, but would be competing with students who all, like her, had nearly straight As, *plus* heavy involvement in philanthropy or sports.

All the schools she chose were top-rated for their marine biology programs She chose California State University Long Beach as her *sure thing*, as she had such a high GPA and SAT score that she outranked most students attending. Of the other two, she couldn't decide which was which as far as her *dream school*, but she knew she had different reasons for wanting each. If she chose UCLA, she would be going to school with Mitch—maybe they would be roommates one day, and their marine biology program was considered exceptional. However, UC Santa Cruz had the highest ranking for marine biology, and she heard the campus and town were beyond gorgeous.

After submitting her applications she put ads at her current school, local high, junior high, and elementary schools for private tutoring in any subject. She had aced them all in high school and her first semester of junior college, so why not?

Before she knew it, she had nearly every block of free time filled, either with driving her grandma or tutoring students, for which she was able to charge $20 per hour.

Mitch hadn't wanted to go back home so soon. He did well enough in his classes, though they didn't interest him very much. He had to have at least a 2.0 average to stay on the team, even as a redshirt. He and Nancy didn't get to see each other as often as either would like, but that only made the time they did have together more special.

He couldn't believe how much he enjoyed the sporting goods store. In fact, he had arranged his following semester's schedule in a way that would allow him to fulfill his entire class load in just two days a week, which would give him four full days at the store. Paddy didn't believe in being open on Sundays, so that was Mitch's only free day, making it even more disconcerting to have to go home.

However, he knew that once he got in his Jeep and headed home, his mind would return to Coach and all he had learned, and he would continue to learn about creating true wealth.

As he threw a few things together—his notebook, the bill for fixing the bumper, and a couple apples, Nancy came into his room.

"Hey, where are you off to?" she pouted, thinking they could go hiking or maybe picnic at the beach that day.

He didn't know exactly what to say. "Wanna do something really boring today?" he said. He figured honesty was the best policy.

On the ride, he told Nancy all about Coach and the sessions. "That's the only part that is *not* boring. Unfortunately, you will have to wait about an hour for me to finish. Coach is very particular that only Amy and I attend."

Nancy completely understood, and figured that he could drop her at some shops or a café first, picking her up after his session. "So, what is so boring?"

"Well, we'll end up having dinner with my mom, sister, and grandma..."

"Honey, why don't we go out on a limb and take them out?" Nancy whined ever so slightly.

"Nancy, this whole thing is about saving money for my investments, so that later on we can go to dinner whenever we want."

She liked the "we" part of his statement. That meant he saw her in his future.

When they arrived in Calabasas, Mitch dropped Nancy at a quaint little strip mall with boutiques and cafés. Thanks to light traffic, he made it just in time to Coach's office.

"I'm really impressed with the progress you two are making," he began the session. "Thinking outside the square is where you will usually find the way to turn your wealth creation dreams into reality."

They talked about their investment strategies and the obstacles they had so far encountered. They also discussed how they had overcome them. Coach gave them some added insights and things to consider as guidance and general encouragement, but in essence he couldn't really fault what they had achieved, given their circumstances.

"Let's look at where you are from a strategic position, shall we?" he continued.

"Think of what we are going to talk about from here on in today as a continuation of the general theme of leverage. See, we are not through with this—the most important of concepts."

Grow or die
a tree can
NEVER STOP
growing and just stand
still; it's either growing
OR DYING.
so is my cash flow,
capital
and ultimately myself
and my wealth.

He opened his manila folder and extracted another handout.

"In the game of wealth creation, *you* have to continually grow," Coach continued, satisfied that his young students had digested the gist of the message. It was now time to elaborate and drive the message home.

"Think of it this way: if you had a ten dollar bill and did nothing with it, what would it be worth in a year's time?"

"Ten dollars," Mitch snapped, feeling cocky.

"Would it really, Mitch?" Coach responded.

"It will be worth less than ten dollars?" Mitch asked, blushing.

"That's right, Mitch. That's absolutely right. But why would that be, Amy?" he asked.

"Because of inflation, Coach," she replied, trying not to look too smug for Mitch's sake.

"That's right. But it's not just inflation, Amy. See, the whole world is constantly moving forward. If you don't invest that ten dollar bill wisely, you could argue that the lost investment opportunities could also be costing you, couldn't you? What I mean here is that if you don't take advantage of the opportunities that come your way, your loss could be even greater because that window of opportunity may not be open the next time you have the chance to invest that ten dollar bill."

Amy pursed her lips together in contemplation as she completed her notes and made sure she had it all clear. "So what you are saying, Coach, is that by just standing still and not growing in value, the ten dollar bill would be losing value simply because of devaluation. But there is, or could be, more to it than that because the economy is growing all the time on its own accord, and this makes the value of the ten dollar bill even worse, comparatively speaking."

"This is why it's important for you to ensure that your investments continually grow. And that's why the projected returns of your first investments look so good, Amy—there's even more you

> Pressure
> for growth to happen,
> I need to be under pressure.
> Sometimes this pressure is
> **NEGATIVE;**
> however with
> goal-setting
> I can make it
> **POSITIVE.**

can do to ensure your investment continues to grow," Coach said.

The twins looked up expectantly.

"You need to add *pressure*."

The blank look in their eyes told Coach they were stumped, so instead of explaining right away, he opened his manila folder and handed out another sheet of paper.

Amy furrowed her brow, her mood pensive. She struggled to understand how pressure could be negative or positive. After a while she spoke, feeling as though she was stating the obvious, "Am I correct in assuming that positive pressure is good pressure while negative pressure is bad, Coach?"

Coach thought for a while before answering. "It *may* be, Amy, but not necessarily. The way I categorize pressure is this: It is negative when it makes you move away from pain and positive when it makes you move towards pleasure."

Amy nodded as she wrote.

"So for example, if you are motivated to begin saving because you just can't stand the constant letters of demand from bill collectors any longer, that is negative pressure. On the other hand, if you are motivated to save so that you can afford an overseas vacation every year, that is positive pressure. Both types may have the same end result—they pressure you into beginning a savings account which is good. The pressures simply come from opposite ends of the spectrum, so to speak."

Mitch followed Coach's reasoning and understood the distinction between the two, but he was having difficulty grasping the need for pressure in the first place.

"Is it always critical to have pressure, Coach? Or does it just happen sometimes?"

Coach leaned back in his chair, scratched Lucy's head, and said, "I guess when you really think about it, you always need pressure, Mitch. See, if things were in equilibrium, there would be no need—no stimulus—to change the status quo. I have always been a firm believer in the idea that in order for anyone to take any sort of action, they need to first develop a greater level of dissatisfaction or a greater vision than the level of resistance they currently have to doing anything. Does that make sense?"

He knew that even for a couple of bright college students, his concept might seem hard to grasp, so he waited to let Mitch and Amy absorb what he had tried to explain before elaborating.

"Think of it this way—why change if things are okay? Things don't usually happen spontaneously, do they? There usually has to be a reason for any action to take place. Everything that happens has to have a cause. Let's take cigarette smoking, for example. Forget why someone may have chosen to start in the first place—clearly many people enjoy it, or it wouldn't be such a huge industry."

Mitch and Amy looked at each other in mock-disgust.

"What's that look for, kiddos? I take it you two are non-smokers?" Coach asked rhetorically.

"Grandma used to smoke," Amy said.

"Used to?" Coach asked, clearly encouraging Amy and Mitch to come up with their own answer.

"Yeah," Mitch said, "she had a boyfriend who hated the smell of smoke, and then her doctor said if she didn't stop..." Coach smiled and waved his hand, signaling that Mitch didn't need to say anymore.

For once, Mitch wasn't embarrassed by his impetuous nature.

"See," Coach said, "everything happens for a reason. Had your grandmother placed a higher value on smoking than her health or her personal life, what reason would she have to change? In fact, what if cigarette smoking wasn't proven bad for health, and what if nobody minded being with someone who did smoke?"

"There would be no reason to change?" Amy asked, but really it was more of a statement.

"Remember, what we are effectively talking about here is *leverage*," Coach continued. "We are investigating the proven wealth creation strategy of achieving more with less. So

Space:
because the law of vacuum
SHOWS ME
that everything grows
to fill the available space,
I need to create space
if I am to become even
WEALTHIER.

before we move on to viewing money in the broader sense, we need to think about one more concept as it relates to leverage—and that is space."

Coach handed out one more sheet of paper.

"The law of vacuum is one of the laws of nature that governs the universe," Coach said. "Like it or not, it governs the way things work. So if you really want to make progress, it's best to take the law of vacuum into account when developing plans, deciding on a course of action, or setting up a strategy for the future."

Amy had no clue what Coach meant. "Can you give us an example of what you mean, Coach?" she asked.

He sat back in his chair with his arms behind his head and thought for a moment. Then after what seemed like an hour, he said, "Think of the last time you cleared out the previous year's fashions from your wardrobe, Amy. What happened?"

Amy smiled and replied, "I filled it up again with new clothes, Coach."

"Isn't that interesting? See, the law of vacuum was at work, Amy. You made the space available for your new clothes. If you hadn't cleared out your old clothes, would you have made those trips to the shops and bought new clothes?"

"Probably not, Coach."

Mitch smiled to himself. "Coach didn't know his sister," he thought. She would be sure to make room for new clothes, although she had done much less clothes shopping recently than in years prior.

"So how does that apply to creating wealth?" Coach asked, eager to stimulate their thought processes.

"How about creating more space for wealth to grow by opening another investment account?" Mitch replied.

"That's exactly what I'm getting at, Mitch. Now before our next session, I want you both to think about what we have discussed. I want you also to see how you can create the space for more wealth to grow for yourselves."

• • •

Amy's tutoring business dropped dramatically when summer came. Not only did her income become practically nonexistent, but her grandma wanted more and more of her time, yet Mom still only paid her $100 a week. Mitch was not coming home for the summer like he had promised, which bummed her out. Once school got out, he worked full-time at the sporting goods store. She eagerly checked the daily mail for letters from the universities where she applied months before, always knowing a thick envelope meant *good*; thin meant *bad*.

This particular June day, her frown turned upside down when she received two big brown envelopes, one from Cal State Long Beach and one from UCLA. She was, as expected, accepted to both. She now waited to see what UC Santa Cruz would decide.

Kim and her team had been on tour with Coach for three long months. Amy started up the porch steps to the home she had spent the last three months renovating on her own as a surprise to her mother. A moment later, a town car approached the house.

"Mom!" Amy ran to the door as the driver opened it for an exhausted, yet joyful Kim. "Oh my God, I missed you so much!"

As the women walked up the steps, arm-in-arm, Kim shook her head. "Three months is just too long!"

"Actually," Amy said, before opening the door, "I have a surprise for you." She put her hands over Kim's eyes, and then walked her into a home she didn't even recognize. They had named this one "The Flop House," due to its condition and proximity to UCLA. However, they couldn't call it that anymore!

Amy had used all supplies from the garage, which Kim had turned into a mini-warehouse for her renovations, as well as everything she had learned about renovating to help and surprise her mother. She replaced stained, worn-out carpet with laminate flooring that looked just like hardwood, but was less expensive and easier to maintain. She had painted the entire interior herself, including all the cabinetry, from dark brown to bright, glossy white. It opened up the entire house.

An amazed Kim began to calculate what rental price the home would bring. She walked around in disbelief that a 19-year-old could transform a home that she would have described as unsanitary (at best) into a charming, clean little "Dollhouse" - its new name.

Kim gladly collapsed on the couch, resting her feet on the ottoman. "Sweetie, you've taken such a weight off my shoulders. Thank you!"

Amy smiled. Over the hours, she filled her mother in on everything she had missed: her two college acceptances, that Mitch would not be coming home for the summer, and that she needed to find something now to bring in more income.

Kim looked around the living room, past the kitchen, out the front windows, which had brand new shades, and she noticed a flower garden Amy had planted to add a final touch.

"Mom," Amy said, at last, "I never thought about what I was going to do come summer, and I've gone from fifteen students weekly to one or two. I need to come up with some money so I can keep investing and still go away to school."

Kim thought for a second. On this last tour, Kim learned even more of Coach's investment "secrets," and she was very eager to grow her real estate portfolio further. With her job, though, she would need plenty of help doing research, viewing properties, hiring property managers, doing the renovations, and everything else that being a property investor entailed.

"Then I say you work for me over the summer," Kim said definitively.

"Mom, I'm not a charity case."

"Amy, this isn't charity. You will be plenty busy, *and* you'll be practicing Coach's lessons on real estate investment. Besides, look at all this - you're a natural!" Kim said, arms outstretched.

Amy felt a twinge of excitement. It seemed like her mom was truly ready to take another step in real estate investment, and now she would get to be a part of it.

"Find a good renter for this place to start, and we'll go from there," Kim said. Her mind worked quickly and decisively, and Amy liked that her mother had an answer that challenged her in many ways.

• • •

Mitch couldn't believe it. He had to go through one more month of football training just to find out if he was going to be on the team the following season. He almost got put on academic probation the prior semester, but Nancy bailed him out. She didn't seem too happy about it, but she tutored him on his writing skills and walked him through a couple of cram sessions for tests in classes he would have otherwise failed.

Nancy walked into the sporting goods store. She was glad that Mitch was alone, and there wasn't a customer in sight. The whole store was like a ghost town after finals week.

Mitch looked up and gave her a half-smile, as he knew what she was about to say.

"I just came to say goodbye. My Uber is waiting outside," she said in her Texas drawl, a tear streaming down her face. She was spending the following two months back home in Texas, and they were used to seeing each other every day. It was going to be hard on the both of them.

A horn blared, signaling the driver's impatience. As Nancy started to disengage from Mitch's arms around her waist, he pulled her back a little, lifted up her chin kissed her softly and said, "You know I love you right?" It was the first time either of them had said it. Nancy's tears quickly turned to a great big smile, and butterflies fluttered around in her stomach as the Uber's horn now blared consistently. She broke through Mitch's grip, walking backward toward the door, smiling ear-to-ear.

"You just said you love me, Mitch McConnell!" she said mischievously, opening the store door halfway, almost like she had something to hold over on him.

Mitch was a little embarrassed. Was she going to leave him hanging? She blew him a kiss and quickly escaped into the Uber.

"Well, I'll be go-to-hell," he said aloud—Paddy's genteel expression for "I'll be damned,"—thinking he'd get a much different response from her.

A few minutes later, he got a text: "I love you too, Mister."

. . .

It had now been four years since Amy and Mitch had first started out on their journey to create wealth. They had just celebrated their 20th birthdays, and they had a lot to discuss with Coach.

The twins had "adopted" Coach as a surrogate father, and they couldn't really remember what it was like not to have him around. Even while he was on tour, they visited him regularly over video conference in accordance with their needs at the time; he gave them tasks, some of which took time to develop and put in place. It was during such times that they found they didn't need to be in touch with him, as not much progress would be made from one session to the next. Then there were times when they scheduled special sessions because they needed to learn concepts or techniques, or because some life-changing event was occurring.

That month after Coach returned from tour was one of those periods.

As they met once again in Coach's plush office, Amy couldn't wait to see Lucy, who was now eight years old and showing a few signs of age. She had a little grey in her muzzle, and she was not as quick as she was when they first met. Over coffee, they discussed Amy's plans. She had not been accepted into the marine biology program at UC Santa Cruz, so it was between UCLA and Cal State, Long Beach. She had been saving as much money as she could, and her mother paid her well for her assistance with the renovations and property investing.

Just prior to the session, Mitch found out some bad news about playing for UCLA. As good as he thought he was, he didn't make the cut. If he kept his grades up, he could still attend UCLA on scholarship and try again the following year. Paddy practically let Mitch run the store, and he paid him an excellent commission and a good salary now too, so that took some of the blow out of not making the team.

"I think it is time," Coach said, without commenting on any of the events taking place in the twins' lives, "for us to discuss in detail my philosophy about money."

They both felt excited to learn more. Maybe they would gain some insight as to where to go from here, not just financially, but otherwise as well.

"It feels like it was just yesterday when we met in Maui for the first time. You two were wet behind the ears and still in high school. Now you are saving, investing, and making some big choices about your futures."

As usual, Coach opened his manila folder and extracted two sheets of paper.

Value add or remove pain the only two reasons people will **PAY ME** in life is that I remove their pain (the more pain the more I can charge) or **I ADD** value to their lives or to a product they want to buy.

"It's now time to start to think a little more laterally," Coach began. "What we have been discussing until now are some solid concepts aimed at getting your wealth-creation-ball rolling. Your first investments are still maturing. We have been putting things in place that will enable you to dip your toes into the investment pool in such a way that your modest efforts have begun to bear fruit in the short term."

Amy nodded in agreement. She and Mitch had indeed taken their first steps and had already experienced the excitement of watching them mature.

"I had begun to wonder if this was all there was to it, Coach," Amy replied. "As you know, we made a handsome little profit from some of our investments, which we reinvested in slightly more ambitious options."

"Yes, but it was really just a case of more of the same, wasn't it? Not that there's anything wrong with that, mind you. Your decision to reinvest in a similar product, but on a larger scale, is great and will deliver you good results as well."

He looked Mitch squarely in the eyes momentarily before continuing. He wanted to address himself now more to Mitch without making Amy feel left out.

"The type of investments you have been involved with so far can be classified as passive investments. I call them passive simply because you aren't actively involved in them. Now because I have classified them as passive, that implies that there must be others that I can classify as active ones, doesn't it?"

The twins nodded simultaneously. They began taking notes.

"There are others that have to do with business. If you are in business, then two very powerful wealth creation strategies are to add value and to remove pain."

They began writing.

"See, when you really think of it, the only two reasons people will hand you their hard-earned cash is because what you are offering them either adds value to something they have or it removes some type of pain they are experiencing."

Coach thought for a moment and decided to give a short example.

"Let's take selling cars, for example. Why would anyone want to buy a car?"

Mitch took the bait. "Because they would otherwise have to rely on public transportation, which is a pain."

"Absolutely right, Mitch," Coach responded, chuckling a bit. A younger Mitch would have said something like, "To be able to catch hot girls."

"Or it could add value by reinforcing their image if it was a luxury car," Amy added.

Coach nodded.

"I'm sure you'll find that if you think carefully, every situation could be thought of in terms of these two factors. And you'll also discover that there is usually a direct correlation between the price they would be willing to pay and the amount of pain it removes or value it adds. Take the car, for instance. This is one of the reasons the market is willing to pay high prices for up-market cars but not for economical ones."

Amy completed her notes, and then looked up quizzically. "So how does this relate to us, Coach?" she asked.

"How do you think it does?"

"Well I can see how it could relate to Mitch, seeing he is working in sales and has a good relationship with the store owner. Paddy clearly wants to be able to come and go as he pleases and spend time with Mitch and the store when he can. But Mitch is basically running the store now, and he can essentially control his earning potential. I think Mitch is not only adding value to Paddy by bringing in more money, but he is also removing pain by letting him be semi-retired." she replied.

"That's perfect, Amy," Coach said, nodding in agreement.

"But what about me? I mean I am still basically just a student," she added.

"Think of it this way: you are now double majoring in marine biology and finance. So when you graduate, you will suddenly be very marketable. You will have a lot to offer any employer, won't you? You will therefore become a great asset to any business that hires you. This means that the amount of pain you will be able to remove for your future boss would be far greater than if you had joined after high school. That's why you will earn more once you graduate."

"Oh, I get it," she replied. "So by double majoring in marine biology *and* finance, I would then be not only increasing my chances of earning more money, but moving closer to my BIG reason, wouldn't I?"

Coach smiled and winked. "You've got it. And besides, there are business opportunities that require both knowledge of marine biology and finance. It's a rare combination you've got going, Amy."

Amy smiled broadly.

"Now while we are talking about education, let's broaden the discussion somewhat. Let's consider the part knowledge plays as far as wealth creation is concerned."

He flipped open his manila folder and handed them each another sheet of paper.

Knowledge:
in life I will
BE PAID
to work from
either the neck up
or the neck down;
neck up pays better
so the more I learn
the more
I EARN.

Mitch started to laugh nervously as he read. What Coach had written struck a nerve after being cut from the football team. Amy tried to make light of it by instinctively laughing too. She knew that Mitch would have loved to make money from the neck-down playing football, but they both knew exactly what Coach was getting at.

She gave Mitch a smile of consolation. They had often argued the pros and cons of further education versus getting an early start in the workforce. She had always maintained that education equaled knowledge whereas Mitch had the view that earning money over a longer period of time would outweigh the initially higher earning potential of a degree. In fact, he was pretty decided on dropping out of UCLA and staying with the sports shop, if Coach could help him think of a way to pull that off.

Amy knew Mitch wanted to drop out, and she really thought that he should try to stick with his studies and not put all his eggs into the sporting goods store's basket.

"We really do live in the knowledge age, but that's not to say that some neck-down activities won't pay well. Some pay extremely well - just think of how much plumbers are earning right now. And, sorry Mitch, but professional sportsmen."

Mitch looked down, somewhat ashamed.

"So what I want you to do now is to go home, and both of you come up with three ways you can build into your future plans what you have learned today. Mitch, what are you going to do from here—the store? Your studies? Both? Amy, you chose UCLA. Where will you live, and with whom? What will you do to further increase your knowledge base? Then, when we next meet, we will discuss your options with a view to setting a clear path for both of you."

The twins nodded. It had been a productive session, and they felt stimulated and refreshed. They gathered up their belongings and made for the door. Their mother had already left to go look at not just one, but two investment properties. If the deals were right, she would use the equity she had in the other investment properties to purchase them.

It was Saturday evening, and Nancy wouldn't be back for cheerleading camp until the following week. Since the store was closed Sunday, Mitch decided to spend the night figuring things out with Amy.

"A penny for your thoughts?" Amy asked playfully.

Finally she got a smile out of Mitch. "Only if you promise to double it every day for thirty-one days!"

They both laughed heartily at that one.

"Seriously though, Mitch, what are we going to do?"

"We?" he asked. His tone suggested that they were no longer a unified entity in any way, now that their lives had gone in different directions and that they were more grown up. Seeing the slightly hurt look on her face reminded him that they were united in a special way - not just as brother and sister, but as twins.

"Do you really want to drop out of school? I chose UCLA mainly because it is a better school, but also to be closer to you. Maybe we could even save money by getting an apartment together if you stay...that is, if you aren't moving in with Nancy," Amy said snidely.

"No, I'm not moving in with Nancy," Mitch said, returning the snide attitude. "I'm not even sure if she'll want to be with me if I drop out. And besides, she's a pretty traditional girl. But if I'm making bank at the store, I'd have no reason to go to classes, right?" He then corrected himself, "I mean, except for you, Nancy, and my other friends."

Amy explained to Mitch that she knew other people who dropped out of school. The result was that they no longer had anything in common with their friends, and after a while they tended to drift apart. She thought that he should stay in school and at least attend part-time.

He hesitated, not sure how he should respond. If things kept going well with Paddy, he'd have a good reason to stay, and he could definitely benefit from taking a few business and sales classes.

"I don't know, Amy, I find myself in two minds. I could just go along with Paddy the way we are and attend school full-time..."

"Or?"

"...Or I could step it up a little bit and make more money with Paddy. I know he's in the mind now to just be with his wife and grandkids. We enjoy each other's company, but he really doesn't want to be obligated to come in. Then yeah, I would either take a class or two or quit for now."

"Wow," thought Amy as she gazed off into the distance. She always thought that Mitch was distracted and losing interest in their coaching sessions, but it was actually beginning to sound like he was learning more than she realized. "That's a huge risky undertaking though, taking classes *and* running the entire business yourself."

"Yeah," Mitch said excitedly, "but I've seen the books now. We have been in the black big time ever since I started with him. He just doesn't want to hassle with it anymore, Amy. I could really make something out of this and rescue him from the pain of dealing with it."

"You have this all thought out, don't you?"

"Well, I mean, he has to agree with it. I'm going to need an employee. One of my friends..."

"One of *your* friends, Mitch? They aren't in the least interested in creating a better lifestyle for themselves right now. They just like to hang out and party." She had noticed this the few times she went to visit him and Nancy for the weekend.

"And what about school? Are you really going to drop out? You could still take classes part time, and *hello*, I could work in the store too. I need the money."

He couldn't argue with what she was saying. He knew deep down that what she was saying made sense. He was slipping back into his comfort zone and was grateful for the wakeup call his sister was giving him.

"You know Amy, it's all too easy to lose sight of the big picture. My investments are ticking along fine, you and I could get an apartment and split the rent, and I can take a class or two to stay sharp in business," he said decidedly. "A lot of it is going to have to do with what Paddy says though."

He jotted down his contingent plan in his notebook and showed Amy.

"This is good, Mitch. I think this scenario is perfect for you. It's not exactly what Coach asked of us, but I think we are on the right track."

...

Mitch phoned Amy that Monday afternoon. "I think we are ready now to go and visit Coach," Mitch said.

Amy animatedly asked, "So what did Paddy say?"

"He said, 'Son, you practically run me store now! Go for it!'"

Amy's shrill scream of happiness startled Kim and hurt Mitch's ear. Looking at her mother, Amy immediately decided that they should convince their mom to buy one for them to live in. From there, they could either get roommates or just keep it as a rental for college students after they left.

* * *

Coach noticed that Kim and the twins had been doing well with their investments, but he also knew that they were still in the beginning stages. Although he did not disagree with Kim's decision to purchase a modest but nicer home just for herself to settle down in, he noticed that the family had nicer things. Mitch traded in his Jeep for a new model, Amy was wearing nicer clothes - he hoped that this wouldn't become a pattern of mistakes. He really needed to reiterate his philosophy on money before delving into the twins' decisions where to go from here.

This was Coach's favorite topic. He loved getting this message across because it was one of the most vital and fundamental ones in his wealth creation arsenal.

It was also the one which was the most fun.

"I love spending money," he began. Amy looked up sharply and smiled. She too had a tendency to be a shopaholic.

> Income rich vs. wealthy it's not just about how much I make, it's what I do with what I make that counts. How much
>
> **I SPEND**
>
> is more important than how much
>
> **I MAKE.**
>
> No matter how much I make, if I spend too much I will always be poor.

"Ever since the earliest of times, the first law of wealth creation has always been the simplest. Remember what I've taught you: spend less than you earn if you want to build wealth," Coach said.

Mitch could hardly believe how logical this all suddenly seemed to him. "I can't believe I hadn't realized this before, Coach. I mean, it staggers me to think of how much I must have wasted over the years. To think how stupid I have been! Buying a new car when the old one worked just fine, spending extra money on Nancy and me going out."

Amy felt proud of her brother; it was one thing to realize you were wrong. It was another entirely to admit it.

"It's not always easy to recognize that which is obvious," Coach replied.

"So what else do you have for us that is absolutely amazing yet blindingly obvious, Coach?" Mitch asked. He really found himself being stimulated and pushed across new boundaries.

Coach smiled and said, "A real entrepreneur knows not only how to make money, but how to spend it. I regard this as your first lesson in entrepreneurship, so make a note of it."

He paused while Amy wrote.

"Here's what I mean. Take two people who've both earned the same amount of money all their lives. Why is it that one ends up wealthy and the other struggles?"

Amy looked at Mitch and replied, "I think it's because one saved while the other lived above their means."

"That's right. You see, money is nothing more than a tool, and when you know how to use it, you'll find hundreds of ways to create instant wealth. But if you don't manage your money, your money will manage you." Coach looked seriously over his glasses.

Mitch liked what he was hearing. Was this the Holy Grail, he wondered? "Just spend less than I make. Simple. Can't wait to hear more about this, Coach," he said.

Coach waved his finger at Mitch, "Now that would be jumping the gun, Mitch. You see, wealth is not just about having a high level of income - it's about having a high level of assets. But that is something we will discuss later. Right now we need to stick to the basics: we need to keep our focus on money philosophy."

Mitch nodded. He knew his sister would once again be laughing silently to herself because he got ahead of himself.

"So how did you do with the homework I gave you last time?" Coach asked. "I hear your mom bought another investment property, one for the two of you to live in while attending UCLA."

"Well, Coach..." Mitch replied, glad at having an opportunity to switch the spotlight away from his shortcomings. Amy opened her folder and handed Coach their homework, which was more a plan of action they intended to execute rather than thinking of three things and choosing one.

"This is terrific, guys," he said, running his eyes down the plan. Mitch had permission to manage the store full-time, and he and Amy would share the home their mother had purchased as an investment property. They would each be responsible for finding a roommate, and they would attempt to charge the roommates enough to cover the mortgage so neither they nor Kim had to pay, or at the very least they would pay much less. Amy, who completed all of her general education requirements in one year of junior college, was now in a great position to take on two majors—and challenging ones at that! The only question that remained is whether Mitch would attend classes the following semester or focus fully on the store.

"So what are you going to do about it, Mitch? School, or no school?" Coach again asked quite seriously.

Amy had anticipated this.

Mitch fidgeted while he thought. He hated being put on the spot like this.

"I guess I'll take just one class next semester...a sales course, Coach, because that will help me with my current job as well as anything I do in the future."

"I like your thinking," Coach replied. "So now I want you to go and research what courses are available, and then when you have selected the most appropriate, enroll and get started."

Mitch nodded. He couldn't believe he was actually being prodded into doing something again. All he could think about was Nancy coming back in a couple days and making the store even better. He felt a little dizzy thinking of all the changes, but then again, that was life.

"That's enough for today," Coach said, rising from his chair. It had been a productive session, and he felt comfortable with the progress his young students were making.

"Give me a ring when you have found a course and made a start, Mitch. Amy, you are doing just fine, and there's nothing much I want you to do right now other than get enrolled in your classes. Who knows - maybe when this is all over with, you can tackle an MBA?"

The twins made their way home in a buoyant mood. Just knowing the plan and getting Coach's approval meant everything to them.

Chapter 9

Mind Your Money

Amy couldn't help thinking about how quickly the time had passed. She had successfully completed her double major, earning bachelors degrees in both marine biology and finance. She would soon begin the MBA program. She had found that as her academic career progressed, she was becoming more interested in the corporate world. The buzz of big business was what she now found stimulating and fascinating. However, she still spent her free time diving. Whether she escaped to San Diego or just buzzed down to nearby Redondo Beach, the ocean was still her passion.

The marine life near the California Coast was nothing like the life in the tropical waters of Maui, but she still enjoyed diving in any ocean. She had also taken a trip with her Marine Biology Club to the Caribbean a year prior, where once again she fell in love with the tropical waters and colorful sea life. She wondered why the Little Mermaid would even consider wanting legs!

Now that she had graduated, she wondered what Coach would think about her taking another diving trip. Would he think she was overspending, or would he think of it as an investment in her education?

For sure, she did need to consider where she was going with this whole marine biology/MBA concoction. She felt interesting and true to herself to pursue two things that had been thematic in her life since the age of 16.

Mitch had always thought that Amy would end up in a multi-national corporation at some point, and felt that the marine biology studies were just a hobby. "Amy, you have the people skills, financial skills, and patience for corporate life," he told her. "I really think that is where you belong—as a CEO of some big corporation." He knew this would suit her, especially if she could find something that utilized her marine biology degree. He found himself becoming slightly envious. She always seemed so focused.

The sporting goods store had become somewhat of a rut for Mitch. He did very well for the store, but Paddy seemed different somehow. Plus, Mitch was ready to start earning some real money. He only took classes here and there, ones he felt directly benefited him in creating wealth. He was not pursuing a degree. Though Nancy didn't necessarily approve of his choice, she loved him and stood by him, even after she graduated. She had no interest in going back to Texas and being away from Mitch.

The twins thought it was time to give up the roommate situation at their mother's investment home, where they had lived since Amy began UCLA. Mitch thought a session with Coach was long overdue. Amy agreed, and they arranged another session for the following week.

• • •

As Lucy painstakingly stood up to greet the two, then circled around twice and lay back down, Coach eagerly jumped into more on his philosophy about money. This, he felt, was one of the most important lessons he could teach them, but they never seemed to have the time over the years to complete this important topic.

They spent the first ten minutes going over the progress they had made toward meeting their homework objectives. Then, satisfied that they were on track, Coach slipped them their next sheet for their notebooks.

"What you have been doing so far is investing in your futures. And you have started doing it early on, haven't you? See, while most people your age have been concentrating on having fun, you two have made a solid start on learning as much as you can about how to go about creating wealth."

I have to invest
TO BE RICH -
I can start with $1 as a child.
I do not have to be rich to start investing, but
I HAVE
to start investing to be rich.

Mitch and Amy couldn't have agreed more, although they had their rare moments of parties with friends. Mitch spent most of his spare time with Nancy, and Amy dove every chance she got.

"And it's not all theory that you have been concentrating on either. You have actually started building wealth through your first few investments, haven't you?"

Again they nodded in agreement.

"You have to make a start somewhere, and the sooner you do, the better because of the compound factor. You really need to congratulate themselves - well done! You are already well on your way." Coach flipped open his manila folder, selected another handout, and passed it to the twins.

"I get the point, Coach; I hear what you are saying. But I really have begun to see the light. I mean, you know that last month I traded in my old Jeep for a new one."

Amy interrupted, "But Mitch you just bought a new one two years ago, so I don't think you see the light. Plus, you and Nancy are always going out, and you buy her stuff!"

Buying stuff
that latest pair of shoes
or "BIG KID" toy is costing me
MY FUTURE.
I need to invest now so I can buy later. Buying all that "STUFF" will mean
NOTHING
to me later in life.
Today's great purchase
is tomorrow's garage sale.

"Please, Amy," Coach said, waving her off, "let your brother finish."

"And I am confident that by the end of the year, I will have enough money from my investments to put down a deposit on my first home. Then I'll have two assets as well as my investments."

Coach let him finish before replying.

"Let me tell you the definition of an asset. Write this down." He wrote on the white board as they opened their first notebooks.

Mitch sat there stunned, then blurted out once again, "But Coach, everyone knows that your home is your biggest asset!"

"And look where it's gotten them, Mitch. Let's take a look at your mother. Her homes *are* her assets. But is everyone who owns a home wealthy? Not by a long shot. The real test of wealth comes from asking yourself this simple question: if I stopped working today, for how long could I support myself?"

Coach let that one sink in for a moment, and then carried on. "Does having a house feed you or eat you? In most cases it will continue to consume your money because you will have to pay your mortgage and electricity bills, as well as for the upkeep and everything else that owning a house demands."

"Isn't that interesting," Amy responded. "I had never looked at it that way before, but I guess it makes sense."

"When you think about it," Coach went on, "most people are quite happy to buy a house, a car and all the 'stuff' they usually do for one simple reason."

He opened his manila folder, selected the next sheet, and handed it out.

"Most people seem to think that if they have all the trappings of wealth—they look rich—then people will think they are rich," Coach began. "They seem to think that it is somehow more important to look rich than to actually be rich."

Mitch was a little perplexed. He kind of liked having the coolest Jeep on the market, and he liked to see Nancy looking pretty in new clothes and a little jewelry here and there. "But Coach, how do you tell that someone is rich if they don't look rich? I mean, surely the only way is by what they have? Like a big house or a nice car?"

> "LOOK RICH" vs. "BE RICH." most people would rather look rich than be rich. **LOOKING GOOD** and having a heap of debt **IS CRAZY.** I call that champagne taste on a beer budget.

"Why is it so important for others to know you are rich? I mean, so what if they can't tell by outward appearances. Wouldn't it be more important to have money in the bank than a huge mortgage? What good will a huge mortgage do for you if you need to lay your hands on some money quickly?" Coach scolded.

Amy could certainly see where Coach was coming from.

"I understand all you are saying, Coach, but I am not sure I agree with you regarding your home not being considered as an asset," she admitted.

"While I agree it makes good financial sense to own your own home outright, and while you still need somewhere to stay regardless, I believe too many people fall into the trap of classifying their residence as an *asset*. Sure, it is in the usual sense of the word, but remember - *it doesn't bring you an income*. And that's what assets should do. Spend your energy on amassing assets that feed you if you want to be truly wealthy."

"But don't assets like cars and houses add to your net worth, Coach? I seem to remember the bank asking me about these when I was inquiring about investment opportunities when we first started," Mitch asked.

"Good question, Mitch. This brings me neatly to the next topic."

He reached for his manila folder once more and handed out another sheet of paper to each of them.

Self worth equals net worth: how **I VALUE** myself will determine how the world **VALUES ME.** I need to work on believing in myself and set my worth.

"It all comes down to how you value yourself, doesn't it?" Coach began. "Some studies have been done that show this to be true, and you can try it for yourself. What I want you to do for homework is to make a list of your ten closest friends. Then I want you to write next to those names how much each of them earns. Or how much you think they are worth, if you like. Got that?"

Amy nodded, wondering if she even *had* ten friends.

"Then add up these figures and divide by ten to find the average. You'll find that your earnings—or net worth—will most probably be around this average."

Amy and Mitch looked at one another, somewhat in disbelief. "Isn't that interesting?" Amy replied.

"I can see that it's about right just thinking about my friends," Mitch added. He was fascinated at what he was hearing and his mind began to race. This was going to be a cool homework assignment. "But how does this knowledge benefit me, Coach?" he asked.

"That was going to be my next question, Mitch. But seeing as how you asked it, let's see if Amy has any ideas."

Amy couldn't help but joke around on this one. "I suppose we need to hang out with a better class of losers!"

Coach wanted to laugh harder than he did. He didn't like to lose his composure, lest anyone not take him and his advice seriously.

Getting back on track, Amy said, "I could begin hanging out with people who are wealthier. If what you are saying is true, Coach, then this would raise my net worth, wouldn't it?"

"That's exactly right, Amy—and by the way, you were right in your previous assessment as well. But do you know WHY it does this?"

"Not really, Coach. It just seems natural that you are only as good as those you hang out with."

Mitch added, "It's like Paddy always says - if you lie down with dogs, you'll end up with fleas...no offense, Lucy."

Coach smiled and reached for his manila folder.

"If you change the way you think ABOUT yourself and change the value you place on yourself both in your head and your heart, you will find that this affects your financial results."

Head plus heart equals wallet:
MY ACTUAL
wealth is an outward reflection of
MY INTERNAL
wealth. What's in my head and my heart will show up in my wallet.

Mitch whistled softly to himself.

"To rephrase, you need to *think* rich before you can *BE* rich," Coach continued.

"This is why the vast majority of people who win fortunes from the lottery or gambling lose it all in no time. They think like poor people, which means they act like poor people even though they suddenly find themselves rich. They spend their money on stuff and not assets. They soon find themselves poor again because their thinking has remained like that of poor people."

Mitch looked at Amy and smiled. It suddenly dawned on him that this was something he needed to work on. Coach sensed what was happening and decided to capitalize on the opportunity that fortuitously presented itself.

"This brings us to a logical end for the today's session," he said, sliding his chair back and standing up. He always made sure to end off on a high note so that his students would have enough momentum to carry them through to their next meeting.

"Your homework is to increase your *internal* wealth. Come up with the ways in which you are going to achieve this. Then, we will monitor your actions to see if it has made a difference."

The twins headed for home on an intellectual high. They couldn't wait to set aside some quality time so that they could hash out some ideas together. In fact, Mitch decided not to go straight over to Nancy's when they returned. He wanted some solitude to really think about the session.

The next morning Mitch and Amy sat down in the store before it opened and resolved to reevaluate their lives from the viewpoint of internal wealth. They knew some soul-searching would be required. Further, they knew that they might uncover some things that wouldn't be comfortable to swallow.

"So where do we start?" Mitch asked. Amy thought for a moment, having anticipated this. She invariably took the lead in such exercises.

"How about we start by making a list of the ten people we are in contact with the most," she responded.

Mitch started off with Paddy. Paddy, from what he could tell, owned one home, a car, and the store. He was probably worth just over a million dollars. He rarely spent money, and his store made a consistent, decent profit every month. Then there was Butt-Broke Bobby Williams who always asked Mitch for beer money. He didn't have anything. By contrast, Nancy did save her money, and not only had she made a few minor investments, she made a major one in a specialty clothing boutique. Coaches at the nearby schools he sold to, who became his friends over the years probably made about what he did, if not a little more. But losers like Bobby, who just leeched off of their parents and held little part-time jobs to buy booze and go out, took his average way down.

Amy thought for a moment. Then, like a light bulb turned on inside her head, she asked, "What about Coach? Do we include him?"

Mitch thought for a moment. "No, we can't include Coach. He will bring our averages artificially up big time!"

They both laughed just thinking about it.

After estimating each set of associates' net worth, they added them together and divided by ten.

When they had done that, Amy said, "So what did you get? My average is $15,000."

"I came up with $28,000."

They discussed their results and concluded that their own income levels were an accurate indication of the circles in which they belonged to.

"What we need to do now is to set a target for how much we would like our levels of actual wealth to be. I mean, we don't need to get carried away by putting down unrealistic figures; we need to stay realistic here because I am still a full-time student."

Mitch nodded.

"I think I should go for $35,000. Is that high enough?" he responded.

"Yes, I think that is fine. And as for me, I think I'll go for $20,000."

They spent the rest of the morning debating how they were going to find new friends to add to their circles. There were some who were doing them no good. Amy had just graduated, and those of Mitch's friends who stayed in school full-time, graduating by the skin of their teeth, were all going to be leaving soon to find jobs or move home. They set a new goal: come up with a practical plan of action and focus in on what they needed to do next to improve their social networks.

Part of that plan was to schedule another session with Coach for the following week.

• • •

That session turned out to be longer than usual.

Coach, impressed with what they had done, told them to repeat the exercise in six months once they had had a chance to establish new circles of friends and influences.

Coach pushed on while he had the opportunity. He said he wanted to discuss a little more about spending money, because once their real wealth started to increase, it would be vitally important that they knew not only *how* to spend it, but also what to do with it.

He started the topic off with another handout.

> Know what to do with it
> the only people who are given the responsibility of a lot of money are the ones who know what to do with it.
> **I MUST KNOW**
> how to invest money and use money
> **WISELY**
> if I want to be entrusted with having a lot of it. It's not good enough to just know how to spend it.

"Money brings with it responsibility," Coach began. "You need to respect it and treat it well if you want it to look after you. Far too many people are flippant about money and this gets them nowhere."

Amy nodded as she finished reading the note. "Like you always say, Coach, 'Manage your money, or your money will manage you.'"

No response from Coach was necessary - they both got it. Instead, he handed out another sheet.

> Only given just enough
> I will only be given just enough money, so I need
> **TO BE SPECIFIC**
> and work out why I need more for bigger and better projects, investments, and luxuries.

"I want you to think of wealth this way: it is a privilege, not a right. You need to be grateful for any wealth that you have been fortunate enough to receive. You need to be aware that you are only the custodian of the money for the time you have it. Use it wisely and make provisions to ensure that those you pass it on to also use it wisely. Money, like your very existence, isn't something to be squandered."

Amy sat in silent contemplation. It hadn't occurred to her to take notes. What she was hearing was so profound that instantly became ingrained in her psyche.

"I have never thought of money in that way before, Coach," she said almost tearfully. She had been deeply moved by what she had just heard. It was as if all of the years of being under Coach's wing had been summed up in one ultra-dense particle of wisdom. "I don't think I will ever think of money in the same way again."

"That's good, Amy. I'm so glad to hear it. And how about you, Mitch?"

Mitch wondered what he was supposed to say in reply. He didn't really get it—at least he didn't think it was as important as Amy seemed to. "Yeah," he thought, "I don't want to waste money, but I have certain things I want, so what's wrong with that?"

Instead, he said the first thing that came off his lips. "This also came as a surprise to me, Coach, but I can fully see what you are getting at. And I agree 100 percent now that I know how I should view money." He leaned back in his chair, hoping Coach wouldn't pick up on his lack of understanding—or sincerity. He had, after all, always viewed money rather differently than his sister had. She was the one who had taken this whole wealth creation thing a lot more seriously than he had. His view had always been more "easy come easy go," but he really did want to change that outlook. "I now see money as more of a responsibility, Coach," he continued. "I don't think I will take it so casually anymore."

Coach was beyond pleased with their responses, which in both cases had been a lot more meaningful than he had anticipated.

"I'm really glad you now see it the way that I do, because it is a serious subject. You see, when you think about it, so much depends on it. This brings me to my next handout."

"The only factor that should decide when you retire, or whether you retire for that matter, should be the amount of cash flow you have, and not your age," Coach said. He waited for their reaction, and when none was forthcoming, he went on.

Retirement is a function of cash flow, not age. I don't have to **WAIT** until I am 65 to retire. I have to wait until I have enough money **TO NEVER NEED** to work again.

"Some people never retire, and this is more likely due to the fact that they can't afford to rather than their not wanting to. Now I know it may seem a long way off for you to be thinking about your retirement years, but the fact of the matter is, you *could* retire in a few years if you wanted to."

This caught Mitch's attention, as Coach looked very deeply into both twins' eyes.

"Yes, he reiterated, you could both be retired by the time you turn 30 if that is your goal. It is entirely possible."

"Now you're talking, Coach," Mitch said, rubbing his hands together. "Then I would be able to spend my days hanging out with Nancy, maybe travel a little, watch some games, have a couple kids, a nice home...how good would that be?"

"I thought that would appeal to you, Mitch," Coach replied. He loved it when his students became passionately involved, though Mitch wasn't getting the entire point.

"So what do you have to do to find yourself in that position?" He asked this question knowing full well that Amy would not be as eager to reply as Mitch was. She would probably just be beginning to fulfill her BIG reason right around the age Mitch claimed so much excitement about retiring.

He paused for a second, not wanting Mitch to reply.

"Let me help you out here," he continued, opening his manila folder as he spoke.

Coach handed Amy her sheet first as a way of ensuring that she remained included in the discussion.

"The secret lies in the second part, doesn't it?" Coach continued. "We all need to earn money just to survive. That is a given. But what most people fail to do is to manage it well. This is what you are learning at college, Amy. Your MBA is ultimately designed to make you into a great business manager. That is why MBAs are usually in such demand, isn't it?"

> Make becomes manage.
> My first job
> **IS TO LEARN**
> how to make money.
> My second is to learn
> how to
> **MANAGE**
> the money I've made.

She conceded, happy she wasn't working her tail off in vain.

"But you don't need to have an MBA to become a great money manager. Anyone can become one as long as they are prepared to learn some of the basics. Then you need to apply them in a disciplined manner. That is ultimately what we are trying to achieve here, isn't it?"

Mitch nodded. He got it—finally.

"I am already earning reasonable money, Coach, and thanks to you I am becoming better at managing it. All I need to do now is to control my debt."

Coach smiled. This comment eased him into the last topic he wanted to touch upon this session.

"Have a quick look at this," he said, passing around another handout.

> Good debt is good.
> I enjoy debt when my debt
> **IS PAID**
> for by someone else or one
> of my investments, but
> **DEBT**
> for my toys or
> "STUFF" is very bad.

"This sums up the exact role debt should play in your lives from here onward. See, you need to acknowledge that not all debt is bad. We really do need to accumulate some throughout life - otherwise life becomes unnecessarily difficult. But you need to realize that there is good debt and bad debt. Unfortunately, most people go through life accumulating bad debt. Your job is to minimize the bad debt and maximize the good."

On that note, Coach ended the session, thanked them for coming, and reminded them to begin working on expanding their networks.

Chapter 10

Cash Flow: Active to Passive

BY their 25th birthday, the twins had collectively done very well for themelves, financially and otherwise. They had, with Coach's help, made many wise financial decisions. They owned their own homes and they both had impressive investment portfolios.

Their new network of friends and acquaintances seemed to reinvent itself. Because Coach made them aware of it, the friends who tended to drag them down wound up self-selecting themselves out, with a little help along the way. As Coach told them once, "Awareness precedes control," so the next time Butt-Broke Bobby Wilson asked Mitch to borrow a few dollars, Mitch simply said no, without any further explanation. Bobby seemed to drift away once he realized Mitch was no longer an ATM machine.

Amy quit a side cosmetics business called "Beauty-in-a-Bag" that she really didn't have time for. She had invested in it anyways because her "friend" Brenda encouraged her to, telling her how much she would make and how wonderful the products were. She convinced her that if she could recruit others to sell the products, not only would Amy make money, but so would Brenda. Amy had to be honest with herself and admit that she did it purely for Brenda's approval, and not because she thought that it was a wise financial decision or something she even wanted to do. As expected, once Amy stopped placing orders—her only "clients" being herself, her mother, and her grandma—she never heard from Brenda again, except for once when Brenda saw her at a party. After having one too many martinis, she told Amy how easy money had come for her and Mitch, and that she really wasn't a "true friend" for giving up the business. She even had the nerve to say that *she* was practically broke because of Amy.

These were the friends Mitch and Amy didn't need. They had no idea, nor did they seem to care, how hard the twins worked over the years to earn the money they had. While these "friends" were out partying, shopping, playing video games, or watching television, Mitch and Amy were usually busy with building wealth. They constantly monitored the market as well as the performance of their portfolios, they went to sessions with Coach or worked on their homework, or physically worked to earn money.

Regardless of any "fun" they might have missed, they never regretted the paths they had chosen. They loved what they did. Mitch particularly loved the notion of taking on the markets and trying to win. For him, this was all a game, and he translated almost everything into sporting terms. Amy studied everything far more diligently than her brother did, and was constantly amazed—and sometimes envious—that he did as well as he did.

Nancy was one friend who always remained true from the beginning.

• • •

After nearly ten years since that day on the beach in Maui, Mitch and Nancy not only remained true loves, but best friends and partners. If Mitch ever needed extra help at the store, Nancy was right there, and she wouldn't even take the money he offered her. "Just take me to the movies tomorrow," or, "Okay, but you're cooking dinner!" was her response. Once she understood more about Mitch's objectives, she even refused a necklace that she knew had been too expensive, considering his goals. She had also become great friends with Amy. Mitch, in turn, had met Nancy's parents a few times, and they hit it off wonderfully.

One night, both families got together for a special dinner at Morton's, courtesy of Fred and Nickie, Nancy's parents. Amy, Mitch, Nancy, her parents, Kim, and Grandma Angie all had dinner together for the first time. Mitch seemed quite nervous, though he had been around Nancy's parents several times before. They were down-to-earth individuals, or what Paddy would call "real people." Mitch already had discussions with Amy, his mother, and Grandma Angie. Now he needed to talk to Nancy's parents.

Between dinner and dessert, Mitch gave Amy the cue. "Hey Nancy, would you come with me to the restroom?" she said.

"I gotta go too!" Grandma Angie, quite spunky in her old age, said a little too loudly. Nancy and Amy helped her up, each young woman taking Grandma Angie by one arm. Amy looked back and gave her brother an approving smile, as she noticed the rest of the party listen intently while Mitch spoke.

When they returned, coffee and a multitude of desserts for everyone to share wrapped up the evening. Mitch gave Amy another signal, and she executed her part of Mitch's master plan. He wanted to ask for Nancy's hand in marriage, but only after getting permission from her parents. He had already discussed this at length with his own family, who wholeheartedly approved. He wanted the proposal to be private, though. He thought, and he knew Nancy would too, that overtly public marriage proposals were not their style. Engagement parties, yes. Public proposals, no. He knew she would want it to be intimate. And besides, he didn't want to put her on the spot. They had never really discussed marriage, but in his heart, he felt he knew that they both wanted it.

As the waiters cleared dessert, Amy told her mother and grandma that she was tired and ready to go. "But..." Kim started, but then when Amy winked at her, she got the clue. "Come on mom," Kim said, helping her mother to the door as the valet pulled around the car.

"I guess it's time for us fogies to get going too," Fred said. He stood up, heartily shook Mitch's hand, and hugged his daughter tightly. Nicky held back tears, as she knew what was about to happen. She hugged both Mitch and Nancy tightly and made a hasty exit with her husband.

Before she knew what was happening, the waiters had placed a lovely arrangement of two dozen red roses on the clean table. Another waiter approached, setting down two Baccarat champagne flutes and a bottle of Dom Perignon, the vintage of which was the year Mitch and Nancy met.

"Mitch," Nancy smiled, not quite knowing what was happening, but knowing it was good. "What is going on?"

With that, Mitch got down on one knee, held a familiar blue box, and opened it. There was no need for a flowery or sentimental speech. As he saw tears of joy fill Nancy's eyes, Mitch felt his usual impetuous self and decided to add some comic relief: "Do you think my girlfriend will like this?"

Nancy laughed, hitting him on the knee. It was a perfect little one carat heart-shaped ring set in platinum. She had always told Mitch that if she ever got married, that was the kind of ring she wanted.

"Well, silly!" Nancy couldn't help see Mitch was holding back his emotions too, "Ask me."

"Nancy Worthington, will you be my wife?"

"Yes, Mitch McConnell," she said in that Southern drawl Mitch loved so much, "I would be honored to be your wife." And with that, he placed the ring on her finger. Those left in the restaurant, who couldn't help but pick up on what was happening, stood up and clapped and cheered as the couple kissed. The lounge singer moved closer to the table and sang "Will You Marry Me?" as Nancy and Mitch danced. It had been the perfect evening.

Now, more than ever, it was time for another session with Coach.

Amy remained single, very much by choice, and had devoted her life to climbing the corporate ladder. She had done extremely well for herself, having been, at the age of 25, the first-ever female Executive Vice President of Finance at her corporation. This was at a marine development and research company, too. She and Mitch both couldn't wait to update Coach on their big, positive life changes.

Kim still worked for Coach, mostly from home unless he had a big tour on the horizon. Otherwise, she spent time on her own property investment endeavors. She had returned to the lifestyle she had with Bryce, but this time it was real. The money was hers, and she didn't squander it on toys. She lived well, and had the things she really wanted and needed, but she always kept a good eye on her money.

When the twins went up to the familiar office, there was one thing not so familiar: no Lucy. When they looked for her in her usual spot under the desk, they looked up at Coach, and his lackluster eyes told all. "Yeah," he said sadly, as the twins stood silent, "we lost her last week. She was thirteen."

The wind automatically disappeared from Mitch and Amy's full sails. They reminisced silently about that fateful night of the rescue in Maui and meeting Coach, thinking now about how far they have come. How Lucy was actually a catalyst for changing their lives.

Coach picked up on their grief, and clapped his hands together. "Just a dog," he said, and he began the session.

"Before we get started, Mitch congratulations. Your mother told me about your impending nuptials. And Amy, great job. A CFO at the age of 25," he said, putting on a happy face.

"With these changes in your lives," Coach said, stepping up to the white board, "it is time for you to begin putting things in place and transition from being active investors to passive ones."

Coach read the first handout of the session aloud:

> Profits are better than wages when
> **I INVEST**
> my wages and time into business, eventually I will produce great profits. Wages are only my training ground for business profits. Profits are about the
> **SUCCESSFUL**
> investment of my hours, not the number of hours I worked.

Mitch flipped open his new, empty notebook—the third one he acquired over the years—and, at full attention, readied himself to take notes. This would be, he told himself, a topic that would appeal directly to him. For some time now, he had been itching to start a business of his own. The sporting goods store still did remarkably well under his management, but Paddy was getting on in years, and he seemed to be losing interest in it. He was convinced that his own business was the next step for him on his wealth creation journey.

"Very few people have ever become really wealthy through a job," Coach began, leaving Amy thinking that she had failed in some way.

"If you want to create great wealth, you will invariably find that it will happen as a result of being in business for yourself. This is for a number of reasons, but mainly because the taxation system is created to favor business owners."

Mitch asked as he scribbled, "Is this the same for any country, Coach, or just ours?"

"Any country, Mitch. You see, when you are an employee, the first thing that happens as soon as you are paid is that tax is taken off. You never get to see your gross pay, do you? So whatever you need to buy has to come out of your post-tax earnings. Basically, whatever is left over after the tax man has taken his share. All governments have a taxation process, and some worse than others."

"I follow," Mitch said as Amy wrote.

"But when you are a business owner, whatever you need to buy comes out of money before it is taxed. The tax man only helps himself to whatever is left over after all your spending on the business is done."

"But what about private spending, Coach?" Mitch asked. "How can we buy private things with pre-tax earnings?"

Coach explained that there was a way to do this, and this is where having a good accountant comes in. "When you are in business," he went on, "you are allowed certain things like incentives for achieving sales targets, board meetings, planning trips, and the like."

He gave the hypothetical example of him and Nancy being directors of their own business. They could, for instance, have an annual sales meeting at some luxury overseas resort. Prizes may be given out. "Now there are certain requirements, like having to keep a record of these expenditures, but your accountant will fill you in here."

Amy, as a CFO, was very well aware of this. It was one of the great attractions of being a business owner, and it was for this reason that she had secretly harbored ambitions of one day opening up her own business. But not yet. She still had much to accomplish in the corporate world.

"So in general, realizing a profit is better than earning a wage," Coach went on. "You see, a profit is not directly related to the amount of effort you put in, whereas a wage usually is. If you get paid by the hour, then there is a limit to how much you can earn because there are only so many hours in a day. Profit, on the other hand, has little to do with hours in a day. You have to work hard for a wage, but not necessarily for a profit."

"So one is active, and the other passive," Mitch said. Coach nodded.

"Yes. Done correctly, profit happens regardless of whether you get up in the morning or not."

Mitch followed Coach's logic.

"So if profit is better than a wage," Coach continued, "is there anything that is better than profit?"

The twins pondered the question but remained silent. It was time for another handout, Coach thought, noticing the new notebooks the twins worked from.

"What about a return on your investment, or, you both probably know this, but, 'ROI?'" Coach prompted as he handed out the sheets.

"When you think about it," Coach explained, again feeling a bit for Amy, "being an employee is all about trading your time for money."

> Return on investment (ROI)
> **BETTER**
> than profits when I reinvest my profits, eventually I build my ROI. Profits are my training
> **GROUND**
> for ROI.
> My ROI is about the successful investment of my money, not my time.

Amy nodded.

"And what is our most valuable asset?"

Harkening back to one of their first sessions, Mitch answered, "Our time, Coach. Because when it runs out, there is no more left and it can't be replenished."

"That's right, Mitch. That is generally why employees are so limited in their earning capacity. But when you reinvest profits you have made through business, you get a return on your investment. You are now dealing with money and not time. And as you will appreciate, money is not a limited resource. It is possible to have an unlimited supply of it. This is not the case with time."

Mitch thought for a moment. There was something that was bothering him.

"But Coach, isn't this a simplistic view? I mean, you are talking about only two things - time and money. But most of us employees use that money to buy assets. Where or how do they fit into what you are saying?"

Before Coach offered his response, he handed them another paper.

Asset rich, cash poor
too many people think that buying assets is most
IMPORTANT.
Ask someone who owns several investment properties, but has no cash to enjoy life.
I NEED CASH
flow first and assets second.

"When you have cash flow, you can buy whatever you need or want. You can have all the assets your heart desires. The trouble is, most people approach this the wrong way around."

"So Coach, is this why you have such a high regard for business? Because through owning a business, you generate cash flow by way of profits?" Amy asked, somewhat rhetorically.

"Exactly. And don't forget that this cash flow is usually passive in nature; it keeps coming whether you get out of bed or not. Of course, it all depends on having a business that can run without you, but that's a topic for another day. Right now, for this discussion, we are assuming that you have a business that has been built correctly, and has been systemized to the point where it runs smoothly without you having to actually be there."

Amy knew exactly what Coach was talking about; she had studied this extensively at college and saw it in practice at her company. It was this specialization that had been responsible for getting her the current position she currently held in the corporate world. By systemizing her department, she had made her name.

"So to summarize all this, here is one final handout for today," he said, opening his manila folder and selecting two sheets of paper.

"Think of your progress on the path to wealth like climbing a ladder. Let's call it a *cash flow ladder*. The higher up you climb, the more you achieve with less effort. This, if you recall from the money house, is what leverage is all about."

> The cash flow
> **LADDER**
> as I climb the ladder,
> I use more and more
> **LEVERAGE.**

"I suppose we have gotten to where we are thus far because of all of our sessions, Coach," Mitch said. "I gather it's all about gaining experience."

"It's something like that, Mitch, but remember, most people never learn as they get older. They just keep making the same basic mistakes over and over again. The trick is to learn; follow what others have done successfully before you. There really is no need to 'reinvent the wheel,' so why try?"

Amy added, "I always tell my employees that every failure is one step closer to success, as long as you learn *something* from it."

"Exactly, Amy," Coach smiled. The woman was wise beyond her years. "So let's call it a day now, shall we?" Coach said. He found that he didn't quite have the same stamina for coaching as he did when he was younger. Regardless, he would see these final clients through. Only fifty-one years old, he felt—and looked—much younger. He was simply ready to change his focus in life. He had told the twins many times that if they participated 100 percent in his wealth coaching, they could retire at thirty, should they want. Everyone was right on their mark, and Coach always fulfilled his agreements. It was a core value.

"Let's do this," Coach said unexpectedly. "I'd like to spend some time on my yacht next week. Why don't you two take a few days off if you can, and we'll do some sessions there. Amy, you haven't lost sight of your BIG reason, have you?"

Taken aback, Amy paused for a moment. "No, Coach," she said. "I love the ocean more than ever."

"Good," Coach said. "And Mitch, I have a feeling we might need to re-explore your BIG reason. I think it may have taken you longer to come up with one, but I'll bet with a little more thought, yours has likely changed."

Mitch and Amy looked at each other, intrigued.

"Nancy would be happy to watch the store for a few days. I'll just have to warn her about Paddy," Mitch offered.

At first Amy thought there was no way she could take off work with such short notice. Then she remembered that her department practically ran itself, thanks to her leadership. "Why not, Coach? Sounds like fun."

They all boarded the beautiful "Tranquility" a week later.

"This is absolutely gorgeous, Coach!" Amy remarked, almost in disbelief that anyone could own such a beautiful watercraft.

"It sure is," Mitch agreed. "And no offense Coach, but wouldn't this be considered a 'toy?'"

Coach winked. "It's one of my favorites. I paid cash for it when I finished a deal five years ago that brought in a few extra million I hadn't expected."

It was time to ramp up the sessions to business ownership, something both Mitch and Amy needed to begin in order to create true wealth.

Coach had his handouts ready. He eagerly jumped into the first topic of the series of sessions that would put them on the path from being employees to being full-fledged business owners.

> Employee
> most people think this is about earning as much as you can, but they
> **ARE WRONG.**
> If financial freedom is my goal, I need to think of this as being
> **PAID TO LEARN.**
> Learn as much as I can.

"When you both got jobs years ago, you may not have realized it at the time, but your education ramped to a whole new level," Coach continued.

"But this is true only if people are serious about learning, as you two were. You see, it's always better to learn in someone else's business because that way the mistakes you made—and I know you both made many at first—didn't cost you your money, but instead someone else's. This bit of knowledge is really only helpful when we assume, of course, that your aim is to one day run your own business."

"But what if you don't, Coach?" Amy asked.

"Then you still continue to regard this as part of your education, Amy. The trouble with most employees is they see the job as an end in itself and not part of the process. What I mean by this is that the whole point of having a job at this early stage in your career is so that you can learn, not earn. Sure the salary is nice, but don't let that mask the real reason you have the job: to learn as much as you can, while you can."

Mitch could understand what Coach was getting at here. He had always valued the opportunities he had been given through work. Learning in "the real world," as he liked to call it. By contrast, Amy had received much of her formative education at college, whereas his had come mainly from the "school of hard knocks."

Mitch hadn't noticed the next handout, which had been given to him while his mind was far away. He jolted back to the present, focused on it, and began to read.

MANAGER

Now i've learned the skill of my job. It's time

TO LEARN

to manage a group of people and resources so that the job gets done and the goals achieved without my doing it myself. It's another level of learning on my path of growth.

"This is where you are right now, Mitch," Coach said. You are managing the store, running it almost independently, but for someone else. Amy operated at this level a few years ago and is now at the next stage, but we'll get to that in a while."

Mitch shot a glance at his sister. He was really proud of what she had achieved, even though he thought the price she had paid was a little high. He certainly wouldn't have paid it. He didn't believe in putting one's career before family. And while he could understand her motivation and reasons for taking the course she had, he still felt deep down that she should have got married, raised a family as he had done, and then gone back to the corporate world if she wanted to. She had to remind him several times that his course was never her dream.

"I'm happy for you, bro," she would say when he started to get into it with her. "You and Nancy have beautiful baby Josh, and now I get to be an auntie again in just a few months. But I have dreams that don't involve any of that - the family I have is enough for me." And then to appease him, since it could happen—she was only in her mid-20s, after all—she added, "But you never know..."

"Really getting to grips with the 'people dynamic' is something that is invaluable in becoming a good manager, and eventually a great leader," Coach continued. "After all, most employees don't live to work. *They work to live*. You two have a slightly different perspective, but ultimately all of your hard work has been for the true goal of freedom for a very long time. Most people don't get this until they are much older, if ever."

The twins couldn't agree more with Coach. Amy remembered the impatience they both had talking about BIG reasons, decisions, motivations, and goals. But now, she saw perfectly how coaching had always kept her on a direct course, and seemingly for Mitch as well.

"Mitch and Amy, as you are now learning, being able to lead and inspire people is one of the most valuable skills you can ever acquire, and it is here that you will learn all you need about how to use it. This will be invaluable when you reach the next level—leadership—because it will enable you to use the principle of leverage to its utmost extent."

Over the years, Coach never missed a chance to instill in them the idea that leverage is one of the most powerful principles when it comes to wealth creation.

"I know, Coach. You can't achieve anything if you can't persuade people to do the things you want from them," Amy chimed in. She had been looking for a reason to enter the discussion, and was pleased that this had come up.

"That's right Amy," he replied. "And you'll find this especially the case when it comes to looking for joint venture partners and the like. But I think we are getting ahead of ourselves here - let's take a look at the level of the leader, like what you are now, Amy, and where you soon will be, Mitch."

He shuffled through the remaining papers in his well-worn manila folder.

LEADER
Now that I know how to manage the resources, it's time to learn how
TO LEAD
the people and get the team to come together to achieve amazing result. Leading is the next level of my learning after managing.

"As I said before, this is where you are at now, Amy. And it's where I'd like to see Mitch before too much longer."

Mitch momentarily pondered what Coach had said just before replying.

"I've been giving this some serious thought, Coach, and I've come to realize that I won't get there in my present job. In any case, I've been thinking about going into business for myself someday soon, and I guess it's then that I'll assume the leadership role."

Mitch explained the situation with Paddy and the store, how he felt all the years in the business would be wasted if he didn't somehow parlay his knowledge, experience and time at the store into the sporting goods business one way or the other.

Coach smiled as Mitch spoke. He had suspected for some time that something like this would be in the cards. "I want to discuss some practical matters about how you can assume a leadership role — we'll talk about this in detail tonight over dinner. I always knew this would be your true destiny, Mitch. And I know you'll do very well when the time is right, and that time may very well be now."

Mitch was beyond ecstatic. He really didn't want to wait until dinner to hear what Coach had to say, but these sessions had become much more casual over the years, and they had become so much more than just Coach and protégés. The three were bonded in friendship and mutual desires—to teach and learn the true concept of real wealth.

• • •

The chef had prepared a lovely dinner of halibut and rice pilaf. There would be handouts, but Coach mainly wanted to have a discussion. As everyone took their places at the table, Coach announced that he wanted to devote tonight's topic exclusively to getting into business for yourself and the stages involved in that.

Knowing Amy wasn't in the frame of mind to go into business for herself just yet, he added, "Amy, I know you may not feel the topic is applicable to you, but it is time for you to start putting into action some things that will propel you to your BIG reason for choosing wealth."

Now he had her attention.

"First, though," Coach started, "Mitch, do you really feel ready to go into business for yourself?"

Mitch didn't have to give it a second thought. "Yes! I've been waiting for this moment forever."

"Well, now, let's not jump the gun. I want to go over some steps towards how to become successful business owners. Amy," he said, pointing his fork at her and speaking before even swallowing the bite he just took, "this is going to be very helpful to you. Mitch, you are a little further along in the course of business ownership, and I am going to let you in on a little secret about working a deal with Paddy. But first, let's just go through the steps of business ownership." It wasn't as if this had come like a bolt out of the blue; it had been bubbling under the surface for quite a few years now. The more Mitch thought about it, the more he knew that he had always wanted to run his own business. It was almost as if he was destined to do so, but the conditions had to be just right. And those conditions, he now realized, included things like the right business idea, the right timing, the right knowledge, and the right amount of confidence, all of which he felt were lined up just right like lucky stars in the sky. Coaching had provided him with more than enough of the latter two.

Coach set aside his folder. The "scrolls," as Amy had christened them earlier in their training, were in the folder, but Coach just wanted to have more of a natural conversation. As Amy and Mitch were no longer children—far from it—a regular, interactive discussion seemed more appropriate at this juncture.

"The first step to owning a business is often through a multi-level business where people recruit others to sell products or services in a sort of 'tiered' level. Get it?"

Amy knew exactly what he meant. Brenda and the home cosmetics business, "Beauty-in-a-Bag," was a perfect example. Brenda had been recruited to sell the products by someone who had invested a few hundred dollars into a "startup kit." She then sold products herself, but also recruited others, like Amy, to invest and sell as well. So Brenda not only made money from her own sales, but from the sales of her recruits, like Amy. As well, whoever had recruited Brenda got a percentage of the profits from Brenda's and Amy's sales. Had Amy been more ambitious and interested in this business, she too could have recruited other salespeople to invest and make sales from which she would profit as well.

> Network marketing business often the
> **FIRST STEP**
> into my own business is through a multi-level business where I have the products and systems provided to me. I just have to learn how to run
> **MY OWN**
> business and, more importantly, how to motivate, recruit, and sell.

"This is where many small business owners start." Coach knew they understood the concept, but he felt it was necessary to say anyway. "It's very often the easiest place to cut your business teeth, so to speak."

"The multi-level marketing business runs on two levels: there's the obvious part, where you earn an income from the product you sell, and there's the not-so-obvious part, where you earn a commission from everything those you recruit under you sell. And it is here that you probably earn the most," Coach continued.

"So that explains why Brenda was so persistent in trying to recruit me and keep me as a distributor," Amy said.

"Yes. The more people you have under you, the greater your earning potential. And when you consider that this form of income will all be passive, you can understand its attractiveness, can't you?"

Amy nodded, but she couldn't quite see herself in that kind of business, nor could she envision herself driving around in the powder-blue Cadillac "Beauty-in-a-Bag" awarded their top sellers.

"Even though you are probably not considering a multi-level marketing business, Mitch, it is nevertheless an important one for many. It can be a great place to begin, especially if you need to start on a part-time basis."

"Is it the only part-time way into business, Coach?" Mitch asked.

"Not at all," Coach said, grabbing his folder, then putting it down again. "A part-time business is a good choice for people who have full-time jobs but want to go into business on the side, like writers, musicians, consultants, and the like."

Part time business it's the step before **I REALLY GO** out on my own, and a favorite choice for tradespeople and consultant types, whereby they do work **ON THE SIDE.** Multi-level marketing and part time businesses can lead to amazing futures.

"Like I said, these businesses are usually started by people that still have regular jobs. Not everyone has the luxury of sufficient funds to get a new business going, so they ease into it rather casually. They get going gently, building up their customer base and an income while they have a job, until they reach the point where the business is viable enough for them to quit and work full time in the new business."

"I guess they wouldn't want to take the risk of cutting off their regular income stream until the new business could support them, right Coach?"

"That's right, Mitch. See, most new businesses can't afford any full time team members in the early stages. They need to develop to the point they can hire employees, and that's the immediate challenge most small business owners face."

"I suppose many businesses start off as a hobby in this way, Coach," Mitch continued. "And then if the demand is there, they turn into full time businesses."

"That's right, Mitch. That's exactly right. And the beauty of growing a business from your hobby is that you'll probably be passionate about it, won't you?"

"Just like Mitch has always been really into sports, so he became interested in working in a sporting goods store?" Amy asked.

"Perfect example, Amy. They could also be stamp and coin shops, model and hobby shops, or even television repair businesses. You, with your love for the ocean and marine life, could do a part-time gig as an aquarium instructor. Help people choose the right tanks, the right fish, and get them started on properly taking care of them," Coach offered.

Amy liked the idea. Chief Financial Officer by day, aquarium consultant by night.

Amy could see how she could become very successful starting her own part-time business—one that truly interested her.

"So let's assume we have this part-time business that has started becoming viable, to the point of needing full time attention from its owner," Coach continued. "What's the next logical step?"

"The business owner quits his job and begins working full time in the business?" Mitch responded.

"So what would you now call him, Mitch? He has ceased being an employee and is now …?"

"Self-employed," Mitch responded automatically.

Coach was already thinking about the next handout as Mitch replied.

"So now you have taken the plunge and gone it alone," Coach continued. "At last, you find yourself really committed to succeeding. You see,

> Self-employed now I've made the step. There is a great deal to learn and master **AS I GROW,** so will the business. This is the hardest step. I need **TO STICK** with it, and remember my first business or two will be more about learning than about earning.

you no longer have the support of an organization behind you; you are well and truly left to your own devices."

"That's what I find scary, Coach," Amy said. "I mean, it would really be up to me to make ends meet, wouldn't it?"

"That's the whole point. Some people find this to be the biggest attraction of all. They call the shots and reap all the rewards. But yes, you are right. It can be scary, especially if you are used to the security of being an employee."

"It's not just the risk of it that scares me, Coach, but the responsibility that comes with it," Amy continued. She wanted to voice her feelings, but she didn't want to dampen Mitch's enthusiasm for starting his own business at the same time.

"And it's not just the responsibility that comes with it, Amy, but accountability as well. Think about it for a minute. You're completely accountable for everything that happens to you and your fledgling business from the moment you open the doors."

Mitch looked pensive as Coach spoke, his mind and pulse racing.

"It sounds like it's all about karma, Coach."

"It's exactly about karma, Mitch. Understand this: karma is the basic universal law that says every action has a reaction, and that every result has a cause. It is one of the basic laws of business, too. So how does it apply to the self-employed person?"

As the butler cleared the dinner dishes, Mitch went on. "If I want to achieve a certain result in my business—say, a turnover of $5,000 in my first week—then I need to take some action to make it happen."

"Very good, Mitch. That's exactly how it works. See, if you take no action at all during your first week other than to organize your office, set up the filing cabinets, and arrange your phone account and email address, then how can you expect to make any sales? You would expect instead to make zero money because you took zero income-earning action."

"But wouldn't it be important to do all those things first, Coach?" Amy interjected. "I mean, you need to have your infrastructure set up first, don't you?"

"Yes, of course you do. but you also need to bear in mind that in any business, there are two types of activities you need to undertake: production activity and income-generating activity. Everything to do with your office, the factory, the stock, the staff, and all that are what I call *production activities*. Marketing, sales, and advertising are good examples *of income-generating activities*. Sure you need the former, but you also need the latter. The trouble with most businesses is that they spend most of their time and effort concentrating on production activities and very little on income-generating activities."

"I see what you mean," Amy said, sipping on a cup of coffee the butler had just poured. She could see that this little exchange had clarified things for Mitch.

"Remember, this phase is still all about learning," Coach continued. "For some people it lasts a much longer than it does for others. Some discover that their learning spreads over a couple of businesses, while others pick it up really quickly. It all depends on yourself as well as your previous experiences and the complexity of the business you are in."

"And I guess for others, the learning process never ends," Amy added.

"That's how I like to look at it. Believe me, I learn new things about business every day." Coach paused to sip his coffee. He had to look through his folder to remember the next step he wanted to cover.

"Oh yes," he said, "managing your own business. If all goes well and you survive the start-up phase of your business, the time will come when you need to start thinking about hiring your first employee."

Coach continued. "And remember, you will still very much be in the learning phase here. You will still be learning at a very steep angle about managing your first business."

Mitch started making a few notes now that dinner was over and they were onto coffee.

Manage my own business now

I'VE GROWN

and employed people,
but instead of managing it
as an employee of someone
else, it's

NOW MINE.

So much to learn,
and I still have to do my
work 'IN' the business.

"Managing people is a very different proposition than managing just yourself. You will find that a whole new dynamic comes into play as soon as you take on your first employee. For many, the fun starts here, and it's also something that makes or breaks them - being able to delegate, to train, to handle different personalities."

Coach paused to let what he had just said sink in.

"You must resist the urge to still do everything yourself. This is usually very hard to do, because until now you have been the one who does everything. You are very good at doing it, because why else would you have gone into business for yourself? You'll most likely find it very hard to 'let go' of some of the tasks you previously did. But you will have to, otherwise you run the risk of losing your first employee. You need to get used to the idea that someone else may be better at doing some things than you are. After all, why else would you have hired them? Personally, I make it a point to hire people who are better at certain things than I am."

This suddenly made such good sense to Mitch. He found himself growing in confidence as dinner progressed. For once, he felt it was all about him and not his sister. She was not, after all, the one contemplating starting a business just yet.

"I can see the difference between running my own business and managing it, Coach," he continued. "But once I've mastered that, should I worry about what comes next, or am I jumping the gun?"

> Leading my own business
> **I'VE GONE**
> from working 'IN' to working 'ON' the business and my years of learning and hard work are starting
> **TO PAY OFF.**

"A very good question, Mitch. Once you've mastered the managing stage, it's time to become a leader. You have gone from working in the business to working on the business."

Amy was quite content to take a back seat here and let her brother ask all the questions, as this was all for his immediate benefit. She was already a leader in business, just not her own.

"What is the difference between working *in* the business and *on* it, Coach?" he asked with a puzzled look on his face. Coach smiled. This was the usual response he received from most of his students.

"Why don't you tell me, Mitch?" he replied.

Not quite sure of himself, he still attempted an answer, "I think working *on* it has to do with the production activities you spoke about earlier, while working *in* it has to do with the income-generating activities."

"No, that's not really it, Mitch," Coach responded. "Working *in* the business has to do with *doing* the work of the business. So for example, if we were talking about a hairdressing salon, the owner would be working *in* the business when she was cutting hair. She would be working *on* the business when she was involved in managing the business, doing activities such as planning, budgeting, setting in place marketing strategies, hiring, and training hair dressers as good or better than herself. Got it?"

"Oh yeah, that makes total sense," Mitch said, scribbling away in his notebook.

"So when you find yourself as a leader in your business, you will be doing a whole lot more working *on* the business rather than *in* it. You will need to be doing this for the sake of the business, because others will be relying on you. You will find yourself having to inspire your team members as well. They will, after all, be looking to you for leadership."

Amy now felt the time right for her to begin contributing to the discussion.

"I suppose it is at this stage that the leader will begin reaping the rewards that come from having a well-trained, motivated, and organized team in place, Coach," she said knowingly, from her own experience as a CFO, but also from wanting to emphasize this point to Mitch.

"That's right, Amy. This is usually where he or she begins to receive some form of passive income from the business."

"Is that because I won't have to do all the work, Coach?" Mitch asked.

"Correct. If you handle this process properly, it shouldn't even matter as far as the results of the business are concerned whether you turn up for work or not. And if you achieved this, then you would in actual fact have graduated to the next level—to that of being a true business owner."

"I have a saying though, Coach, about leadership that I subscribe to heartily," Amy added.

Coach grinned, taking a last sip of his coffee, thinking perhaps the student had begun to surpass the teacher. "What's that, kiddo?" he asked, unable to conceal his amusement.

"Well, 'don't expect what you don't inspect.' I mean, you can have a great team, but don't you think it's important to check up once in a while?"

"Very good point, Amy," Coach admitted, "but you will find that as time goes on and the business continues to prosper, less and less 'inspecting' will be necessary."

With this last interaction, Coach decided to postpone the conclusion of the business ownership discussion until morning. He had a brilliant idea for Mitch's sporting goods business, and he wanted to sleep on the impending conversation. He handed each of the twins each the set of handouts they had discussed, bid them goodnight, and proceeded to his cabin.

• • •

The next morning Amy, so comfortable now around Coach, stood in a plush terry robe, leaning on the rails as they sailed away from the sunrise. She held a cup of steaming coffee in her hand and two worlds on her mind: the one above sea level, and the one below.

Coach startled her out of her deep thoughts when he put a hand on her shoulder and said, "A penny for your thoughts."

That had been an ongoing joke between the three of them for years now.

"Let's see," Amy said, with deadpan humor, "you know, I think I'll just wait thirty-one days and let you give me the $10,737,418.24."

"Hmmmm," Coach rubbed his stubbly chin, "still thinking about that aquarium, are you? The BIG reason?"

She hadn't expected his response, and she found it uncanny that he appeared to read her mind.

"You know, Amy, you have invested your money very well over the years. But you are still an employee. Even if you become the CEO, and I have no doubt that you will if that is what you want, you will still be an employee. This BIG reason of yours is a very positive one indeed, and it can also be the catalyst that makes you a very wealthy woman. However, you are going to need people who believe in you, and you have many who do. Of those many, you will need to seek those who have the venture capital to invest so you can build that aquarium and tackle your marine conservation efforts."

"Wow," Amy thought. She always wondered how she would go about realizing the BIG reason. Yes, she made a great salary, but even if she saved 15% of her earnings over the next five years, she would still only have a quarter of a million dollars set aside. An aquarium like the one she dreamed of—where people from all over the world visited to learn about and see ocean creatures from far and wide—would cost at least $40 million, perhaps more.

Coach winked at her. "You never know - I'm one of your biggest fans. Maybe I will give you that penny for your thoughts after thirty-one days."

Before she could even digest what Coach had just said—was he serious?—Mitch walked up to the deck, sleepily rubbing his eyes.

Everyone said their good mornings, and Coach, eager to finish this session and return home to his family, instructed Mitch and Amy to first grab a bite of the breakfast the chef had prepared, and then afterwards to meet in the salon.

...

With everybody freshened up and ready to roll, Coach went right into the conclusion on business ownership, this time handing out scrolls first.

> Business owner now that I've bought back my time,
> **MY TEAM**
> runs the business, and I choose whether I work, play, or do a bit of both. I have a passive cash flow; I've made it to
> **THE TOP**
> of the cash flow ladder for the first time.

"The business owner will now, perhaps for the very first time, really start reaping the rewards of being a business owner," Coach continued.

"And if you bear in mind that the economy is constructed to suit business owners, then this is quite something. Being on top of the cash flow ladder is a great place to be because this is one of the only two ways in which you grow real wealth. The other is the capital ladder."

Amy had something on her mind. She shot a quick glance at her brother to make sure he wasn't about to speak, and when she saw he wasn't, she cleared her throat.

"So Coach, when the business owner gets to the stage of being a 'business owner,' does he stop being one in order to take the next step by getting on to the capital ladder?"

"No, Amy, what happens is that he climbs the cash flow ladder again and again, which brings me to our next topic," he said, handing out a final sheet as the yacht pulled close to shore.

> Climbing the ladder
> again and again over time
> **I WILL CLIMB**
> bigger and better ladders
> that produce even more
> monthly passive cash flow.
> The difference is, now
> **I KNOW**
> a lot more
> about what I am doing.

Amy quickly read the handout and nodded. "I'm with you, Coach."

"I know you are, Amy," Coach said, seeming a lot more sentimental than usual. "I know you both are. I can't tell you what this experience with the two of you has done for me. You see, my BIG reason for choosing wealth was to pass on my knowledge to help others create abundance throughout the world. I don't know two people more worthy of such than you two. It may be awhile before we see each other again, but I'll be a phone call away if you ever need me."

The twins, perplexed, had not expected Coach to make such a farewell. It was as if he was a mother bird, pushing his chicks out of the nest because he knew it was time for them to fly. He gave no explanation as to how long it would be before they reunited again or why it would be for "some time," but they didn't ask questions.

As Amy and Mitch started down the stairs to gather their belongings, Coach called out to Mitch. "Come here, son, I'd like to have a word with you. Amy, I'll see you when we disembark."

Mitch stood by the railing, feeling nervous for some reason. His legs felt shaky, and he felt flushed. He always wished that he didn't blush or get flushed, but he couldn't help it. The more he tried to suppress it, the worse it got.

"Let's sit down," Coach said, motioning to a canvas bench.

The two men sat - no notebooks, no papers, just the two of them, one-on-one.

"You've devoted your life to that store," Coach began. "You did it because you needed the money at first, but sports has always been your passion."

"Yes, Coach," Mitch agreed.

"So you have this situation with Paddy, the owner. He is your friend, and in a way, your business partner. And he is getting on in years and doesn't seem interested in the business anymore. In fact, from what you've told me, he may be in trouble."

"True," Mitch nodded.

"My idea is this...rather than starting from scratch with your own store, offer to take the lease over for Paddy in exchange for complete ownership in the store. You have built great relationships with your vendors and customers over the years, so the vendors will probably give you the same credit terms Paddy has. Otherwise, maybe Paddy will just be a silent partner for a time. Either way, you will become the business owner. Now, you may need to negotiate with him. He may still want a monthly percentage of revenue or a cash buyout up front. There are many possible scenarios, but I believe you can do this. Just don't give him more than $10,000 up front or 5% of the revenues, as you will need to invest in employees, inventory, the lease, utilities, et cetera. And ownership must be transferred to your name."

Mitch, overwhelmed, couldn't wait to get home, run some numbers, and when the time was right, make a proposal to Paddy.

As Amy emerged from the stairs and the yacht had pulled into the harbor, Mitch stood up and shook Coach's hand. "I don't know how to thank you, Coach," Mitch said, choking up a bit.

"Yes you do, son. Yes you do," Coach said, looking him eye-to-eye. "Well, guys, I'd like to thank you for coming along with me. I like to take this old gal out every once in a while, and you both made it really special." Coach also wanted the show them that, yes, it really was okay to have luxurious toys—boats, cars, homes, and such, as long as the proper steps were followed and they were purchased for the right reasons.

It had been a good, inspirational trip with Coach. Mitch now felt perfectly comfortable about what was ahead for him. They gathered their belongings, thanked Coach, and headed to the speedboat that would take them to shore. The time for taking action was here, for himself and his sister, Mitch knew. They waved goodbye until Coach was no longer in sight, and they went ashore.

• • •

Mitch knew that he was on his own with Paddy. Coach had given him more advice than he probably wanted to, and Mitch knew it was because he wanted him to figure it out for himself—based on his years of coaching, of course.

Negotiating with Paddy wasn't hard. They, too, had become true friends, leading Mitch to believe that whoever said, "Don't mix business with friendship" was dead wrong. There certainly are *caveats* involved, but true friends might just be the best people with whom to do business, Mitch thought. This was certainly the case with Paddy, because trust, honesty, and genuine regard for the other's best interests were at hand.

Paddy, at nearly 80 years old, loved sports and loved the business. But he wasn't just tired - he had a very sickly wife, and his drive to accomplish any more than he already had in business had subsided with his youth. His own children had no desire to be part of the business. Mitch had been a friend, a tireless worker, and in a way, a savior. Paddy hadn't known when he hired Mitch why his wife had stopped being his business partner. He didn't know how sick she was. Now he did want out, but with contracts with vendors and three years remaining on his lease to fulfill, he couldn't just close the store, lest he wanted to die bankrupt.

Mitch, prepared to pull any of Coach's tricks out of his hat, approached Paddy with an offer to buy the store. For the first time in years, Mitch saw a light in Paddy's eyes.

"I know you love this store, Paddy," Mitch said. He sat down with him for the first time ever, over a beer and a shot of whisky. Mitch wasn't much of a drinker, and he certainly didn't want to take advantage of Paddy, who was. "And I also know you need out of it," Mitch smiled kindly.

For once, Paddy didn't argue with him. "I'm listening, Mitch," is all he said, as he sipped his whiskey.

Mitch, an excellent reader of people, knew that by simply sipping his whiskey and beer, Paddy took what Mitch had to say seriously. Likewise, Mitch drank with Paddy, because he had been told by Paddy and others, "Never trust a man who doesn't drink," probably meaning one who won't at least order a drink and sip it with you.

"What if I were to buy the store from you?" Mitch asked in all seriousness.

Paddy laughed, spitting a bit of his beer.

"Jeez Paddy, I wanted the news, not the weather," Mitch frowned jokingly, as he wiped his arm. Paddy kept his falsetto laugh going until he finally could contain himself.

"Mitch," Paddy said, "I love you like you were me own son, but you don't have the money to buy that place. Jesus, I don't have the money to buy myself out, or else I would. I've got a lease, and vendors I'm obligated to...."

"Paddy, I've got a solution," Mitch said, sipping his Guinness. "What if I take over the lease, and I am responsible to the vendors. You transfer the store into my name, and give you a monthly share in the net revenue? My credit is good, and if I have to, I can put some money down. While I'd rather not, you would be completely free from the store."

Mitch had Paddy's full attention.

"If I get everything transferred to my name, your only risk is a percentage of revenue, and you have already told me you would just close the store now if you could," Mitch added. "So, what are you risking?"

Paddy tapped the cocktail waitress on the behind, something that only Paddy could get away with because he had been a customer for so long, and he didn't know any better. "Honey, get us two more of these," he said. One thing Mitch learned from Coach is that if someone either offered you a drink—whether it be iced tea or whiskey—they were willing to negotiate.

"I'm listening, lad. I'm listening."

Mitch knew the ball was now in his court. He wasn't about to screw Paddy over, but he also left the emotion out of the deal. It was a difficult thing to do, but he had been well-trained. Mitch harkened back to the first time the two met, when Mitch propositioned Paddy for the part-time work.

"Okay," Mitch said, "here it is. You sign the lease, the contracts, the utilities, and the entire business over to me, and I'll give you a percentage of the monthly net revenue."

Paddy looked intrigued, and happily so.

Mitch knew what he had to do to close the deal. He playfully grabbed Paddy by the wrist and said, "But I'll tell you what, old man, you're not getting a penny over five percent, and if I catch you stealing as much as a golf ball from me, I'll cut off your hand!"

Paddy laughed heartily. "Laddie," he tried to stop laughing long enough to speak, "I would've given it to you for nothing!"

That night was a "handshake" deal, but the next day, Mitch, out of due diligence, had attorneys draw up the papers. He and Paddy approached the landlord about signing the lease over to Mitch. Relieved that Mitch wanted to take over and having seen the books over Mitch's years of almost singularly managing the store, he readily agreed to transferring the lease. In actuality, they had been a bit nervous that Paddy would kick the bucket before the lease was up, and what then?

When Paddy was out of earshot, Mitch negotiated with the landlord just prior to signing the new lease. "See, I just bought this store, and I'd like to make some improvements," Mitch said. "I want to get some stock in here that is a little more modern and some better signage, which will attract more customers to the block. But to do so would take up all of my remaining funds, so I do agree to take over Mr. Ryan's lease, but only on the condition that I have a rent-free period the first six months of the lease." This, Mitch knew, is what Coach meant whenever he spoke of "creative financing."

The attorney looked at the landlord and shook off the deal.

"No deal," the landlord said, insulted and about to leave the building.

Mitch purposefully looked over at Paddy, who may as well have been singing "*Tiptoe Through the Tulips*," as he skipped down each aisle, saying, "Goodbye t-shirts, goodbye jockstraps, goodbye baseballs, goodbye bats," and so forth.

"I apologize Sir," Mitch said, once again looking over as Paddy raucously bid every item in the store farewell, "I was working under the assumption that you would much rather the business do well than struggle or even stand empty. What would that do for all the other tenants in the building? It wouldn't be good for business overall, would it?"

Both the landlord and the attorney became a little pale with Mitch's counter-offer combined with Paddy's antics.

Mitch went on, "Now I'm not trying to get out of paying the rent at all; I will simply pay the first six months of rent at the end of the lease."

Mitch raised an eyebrow to the concerned-looking landlord. "Or, we could just see what happens with Mr. Ryan. It's up to you. But if you ask me, it looks like he's already checked out."

The landlord and his attorney whispered to each other, and the landlord, nearly cowering, countered softly, "Three months."

Mitch smiled victoriously and put his hand out to shake the landlord's hand, "Four it is then!"

Mitch figured (according to Coach's instruction) that if he sold the business, the few months of free rent would buy him some time to build up the business again, and he could sell it for a better profit. However, Mitch really wanted to make a go of the store as his own first business. He contacted vendors of some popular smaller items like golf balls, socks, headbands, and other giveaways, in exchange for an in-house promotion during the grand opening of "McConnell's Sporting Goods." He also asked neighboring tenants to provide hors d'oeuvres and wine in exchange for the same in-house promotions. With Nancy's help, they contacted everyone in the database and invited them to the grand opening night, which went off very well indeed. It wasn't long before the books looked better than ever.

It was now eight years since Mitch opened the doors to his sports shop, and life couldn't have been better.

Chapter 11

The Beginning

In the meantime, Amy's career had soared to new heights. She now held the CEO position in a multi-national scuba diving equipment, certification, and charter company. This involved extensive overseas and interstate travel. She loved the travel, although traveling on business was not nearly as glamorous as she had always imagined. In spite of this, she loved the fact that she got to meet new people and dive in new seas constantly. It was her life. She didn't ever stop to think about settling down. Dating and having fun with friends around the globe suited her to a tee.

For all intents and purposes, Coach, now nearly sixty years old, was retired. He felt that he had spread his knowledge around enough. Through his books, seminars, private clients, and his own children, his idea of an abundant world through wealth education would go viral. Now it was truly time to enjoy the bounty his life's work had brought him, which included his family and friends.

Kim retired along with Coach, both promising each other they would stay in touch, and Coach said, "I really believe Amy and Mitch have learned what they needed from me. If they didn't, they will find their ways. However," Coach told Kim, "I'm only a phone call away. For them and for you. Always."

At 68 years old, Kim had certainly built up her wealth. She had moved to Calabasas, where she put Grandma Angie into the most luxurious retirement home in the area. The property investments over the years, plus some other paper investments, had her living a life of luxury she had truly earned. Though taking care of her mother could have easily been considered her "BIG reason," she still felt there was something missing.

• • •

One thing Mitch and Amy tried to do, thanks to Nancy and her upbringing, was celebrate special occasions as a family. Before they became wealthy—and Mitch and Nancy were at different levels of financial wealth than Amy or their mother—Christmas might mean a potluck with both families (Nancy's and Mitch and Amy's) and lots of little toys for the kids. The kids always got savings bonds or some sort of investment as well, but they were too young to know what that meant. So the family tradition was for all the adults to throw in $100 a piece and have a field day at Toys R' Us. With Grandma Angie, Kim, Nancy's parents, and Mitch and Amy, each could fill a cart of games and toys the kids would get a kick out of opening. Nancy could, and without guilt, spend more on the wrapping of the gifts, which she enjoyed more than the gifts themselves. Afterwards, the adults went out together to dine and drink great wine while the nanny watched the kids. The real gift, however, was an investment they all put together for each child.

As everyone got older, the celebrations got a little bigger and more extravagant, but Mitch and Nancy's children were not to be spoiled by "toys." Instead of a $10,000 hover board, for instance, one birthday Josh got an X-box, as well as a $50,000 piece of undeveloped land that everybody figured, after extensive research, would be worth approximately one million dollars in just ten years. Apparently, all the road construction they witnessed on a desolate piece of highway was intended for a private airport for an overnight shipping company and an online warehouse.

Now, on their 40th birthdays, Mitch and Amy decided that they would be even more extravagant than they were comfortable with and take the family to Las Vegas for the party of a lifetime. Kim was in charge of booking them into suites at the only five-star resort in Las Vegas, all adjoined and with private pools overlooking the golf course.

As Mitch got in his first game of golf, the very first thing he had wanted to do in Las Vegas, he thought for a moment about how grateful he was to Coach. They had thought of inviting him, but after some consideration they decided they didn't want him to feel obligated. After all, he had his own family vacations. It was a tough decision, and as Mitch played within a random foursome, he couldn't help but think about how great his lifestyle had become, and yet he didn't have a Gulfstream or homes everywhere across the globe.

Genuinely happy, he still wondered how Coach attained the level of wealth he had. While Mitch was definitely rich, he realized, with a twinge of guilt, that he became rich just to be rich. His BIG reason—to care for his mother and grandmother in their old ages—did not exist anymore. He looked around, noticing several men with their young sons, playing at one of the most beautiful and elite courses in the world. He began to feel for the kids who would never have this opportunity - kids who grew up in poverty, or simply lacked the support they needed to facilitate their athletics. He had begun, at the age of 40, to really think about his true BIG reason. He planned on exploring it more with Amy when they returned home.

They chartered a private plane to Las Vegas and arrived at the resort by limousine. They were all so excited! The flight was good and the weather fantastic - they couldn't have asked for better. The party was scheduled for their second day in Las Vegas to allow the children to acclimatize and settle down. They had never seen anything like Las Vegas or the resort before.

Business was far from their minds as they made their way to La Cave, the restaurant at the resort they booked for the birthday celebration. Amy visibly began to unwind and Mitch looked fitter and more purposeful than he had in a long time. Their mother commented on how good they were looking. It was just like old times, but better, she said.

• • •

There was much joy and laughter around the restaurant that evening. Coach's advice about rethinking their circle of friends had certainly been good. They simply showed up on their own, with a few hints from the parents that there would be a birthday celebration.

It had indeed turned out to be an event they would remember forever.

Mitch and Amy had never been inside a casino before, and they wondered what it would be like to play for a bit.

"What do you want to try?" Mitch asked, as everyone at the party danced, drank fine wine, and ate tapas amidst a lamp-lit Old European atmosphere. "C'mon, nobody will notice if we sneak out for a minute."

Amy wanted to play a slot machine. She picked one with a mermaid theme. Semi-reluctantly, she pulled $20 out of her purse. She pushed the button one time, but really didn't know what she was doing. A casino representative approached her and said, "Miss, I really shouldn't tell people how to gamble, but I noticed you aren't playing all the lines. I wouldn't want to see you hit it and not win," the kind woman said. She had noticed how excited Amy was to play a slot machine.

"I just don't know what I'm doing!" Amy exclaimed.

Being very careful not to say anything that might cost her her job, the representative said, "Well if I were to play, I would play all five lines at 25 cents apiece. It's the maximum bet, but then you won't be disappointed if you either win and have bet too little or a line you didn't play wins."

"So," Mitch said, "in total, her bet is $1.25 per spin."

As a birthday present, Mitch gave Amy a $20 bill to try the machine some more. She ended up getting five of the dark-haired mermaids, which apparently triggered the machine to give ten free spins. Amy jumped up and down with excitement as Mitch looked on, happy to see his sister so thrilled. He had never played a slot machine either, but he was just happy for his sister.

At the end of the "free spins," she had won $120 from only $40 invested, with a total cash out of $156. She pushed the button, took the voucher for $156, and couldn't have been more thrilled than if she won a home or a car.

The only other person who spent any time gambling after Amy's first and last foray at the slot machine was Grandma Angie, who had a great time playing nickel slots and sipping on mimosas for much of the vacation.

Amy decided to give Mitch and Nancy a day to themselves so they could take Kylie and Josh to the Shark Reef at Mandalay Bay. The three were in awe at what they saw. The smaller exhibits showcased some unusual (and very poisonous) fish, and the huge aquarium filled with several shark species delighted them greatly. They were particularly excited to see the largest aquarium of all, where sea turtles, a sawfish, halibut, and many other sea creatures lived. Amy had seen many of these species on her many dives, but this was Kylie and Josh's first experience with such marine life.

"Auntie," Josh pointed, "why does that big turtle have a floatie on his back?"

Amy looked twice. Indeed, the sea turtle did have some type of device attached to its back.

The docent overheard and answered Josh. "That is Oscar. Many of our fish and other creatures are rescued. We take sick animals like Oscar, who had a breathing problem and would have died in the ocean, to special veterinarians who specialize in marine life. They fix them up if they can, and then we keep them here to make sure they get proper care.

Amy, very pleased, felt it was time to go for her BIG dream - the aquarium. She had amassed enough wealth with her investments, including the one she had first thought of as a mistake: the $5,000 she invested at age 18. She meant to leave it for a year and then reinvest it, but because so many other opportunities had come along, she decided to leave the $5,000 alone. Over the years of working, investing in property with her mother, and other investments Coach taught them over the years, the $5,000 slipped her mind. It was now worth tens of thousands of dollars.

Ten years as the CEO of the marine research and development firm was truly lucrative, and she figured that she had amassed the wealth she needed to retire and have the lifestyle she always dreamed of. Now, she could turn her attention to her passion for the ocean—the conservation efforts, and of course, building the aquarium.

The remainder of their short holiday was spent as truly quality family time: swimming, laughing, relaxing, shopping, dining in fine restaurants, and just enjoying the reunion. Amy and Mitch did get together one night for a glass of wine and some appetizers—just the two of them.

"You know, Mitch?" Amy said, sipping her vintage cabernet. Mitch couldn't help but notice what a lovely woman his sister had become. She could have been a model like their mother, but instead here she was, a wealthy marine biologist with an MBA and CEO of a company that needed someone with both credentials.

"Yeah, sis?" he asked, toasting to her.

"I've been thinking..." and she explained how the trip to the Shark Reef with the kids reminded her of her BIG reason, and that she now felt ready to retire and concentrate on her BIG reason.

Mitch confessed that he, too, had rethought his BIG reason, and he wanted it to have something to do with underprivileged children and sports. He also discussed a little about how he knew they had become wealthy, but he wondered if they would ever be as wealthy as Coach.

Amy noticed his blushing, and she felt a little perplexed that Mitch didn't feel like he was quite wealthy enough. However, just because she was content with the wealth she had amassed didn't mean he had to be.

Maybe it *was* time for one more visit with Coach. It had been several years.

Chapter 12

The Middle

Amy and Mitch drove together in Mitch's Lamborghini to Coach's new...actually, they wouldn't even call it a house. It was more like an exquisite compound, complete with a guard-shack, beautiful wrought-iron gates that incorporated the letter "C" throughout, and pebble drives with smaller guest and servant homes leading to the main home. It was a veritable mansion on the sea.

A butler in formal uniform opened the door, where he showed Mitch and Amy to the parlor.

"Mr. McConnell, Ms. McConnell, may I offer you a beverage?" the butler asked.

Mitch and Amy declined, noticing there was a pitcher of water and a few elaborate snacks already set out on the coffee table.

A familiar voice rung out: "So how are my two favorite students?" Coach appeared at the top stair of the sunken-parlor. "That will be all, Gary," Coach said kindly to the butler, "thank you."

Amy figured Coach was nearing seventy...maybe only 66 years old. However, he still looked young. The laugh lines around his eyes had deepened, and his dark brown hair had gone grey, but he seemed just as spirited and peaceful as he ever did.

Mitch filled Coach in about the trip to Vegas, and Amy relayed her decisions regarding retirement and her BIG reason.

"It's always good to see you - after all, it's been years. But now—and please don't feel embarrassed—I know that two busy millionaires like yourselves didn't just stop by for a friendly chat. Not that I wouldn't mind that once in a while, either."

They both blushed as though they were 16 again, sitting in Coach's office across from him at his desk.

"Come on kiddos," Coach chuckled, "let's have at it."

He still called them "kiddos" at 40.

Mitch explained, as graciously as he could—and he did, as he had become quite the gentleman—that he was grateful for the wealth he had acquired under Coach's tutelage. Like Coach had said, he could retire by forty if he wanted to. But the thing was, he wasn't ready to do so yet. He then became perfectly frank about wanting to do whatever it took to reach Coach's pinnacle of success.

Waving his arm around the room, he stated, "I'm sorry if I sound shallow, but I want all of this. And I also changed my BIG reason for being wealthy to not just include having beautiful homes, cars, yachts, and such, but I want to have the money to give *all* kids the chance to play sports, whether they can afford equipment or fees or whatnot..."

Coach, very pleased, said, "Sit down Mitch. I had a feeling you two would be back one day. He rang for Gary to bring in "an old ratty manila folder from the top shelf in his office."

"What we are going to discuss today is the concept of the cash ladder," Coach went on. "But I think a quick recap is in order."

He opened his file, flipped to the summary sheet at the front, and quickly scanned its contents.

"When we first began delving into the whole subject of wealth, I asked you to consider why it was that you wanted to be wealthy, didn't I? Then I explained the money house, but I only talked briefly about the capital ladder."

"Right," Mitch said.

"Now what I want to do is to go into the capital ladder in more detail." He opened the well-worn, almost grey folder and chose two more "sheets of wisdom." He handed them to Amy.

> Cash flow physical assets and paper assets: when I have completed or started making significant cash flow from
> **MY CASH FLOW**
> ladder, it's time to learn how to start investing my cash flow
> **INTO**
> firstly more cash flow, secondly physical assets, and thirdly paper assets. And then to do it!

"Once you have started to generate cash flow, and I understand that is now the case with both of you, you need to decide what to do with it. You can blow it on stuff, or you can use it sensibly to add to your wealth. Those are the options we will be talking about today."

Amy began to take notes. Mitch, quite content, listened for the time being. He never wrote if it wasn't necessary, and Amy took great notes anyway. Besides, his mind was like a steel trap—he remembered everything.

"When you think about it, most people end up asset rich and cash poor," Coach continued. "They approach wealth creation the wrong way around. What they should be doing is developing their cash flow first before worrying about investing in fixed assets like real estate. Once you have a good cash flow stream, you can do anything you like with it. All you need to do is decide what it is you want to do. How much fun can that be?"

"Yes, I know exactly what you mean, Coach," Mitch said. "I have seen it all too often and, I have to admit, I have been prone to falling into that trap myself."

"You need to steer your excess cash flow when you have it into avenues that are likely to generate more cash flow first, because as you now appreciate, cash flow is king."

Amy looked up, intrigued.

"Once you have developed your cash flow through reinvesting your surplus cash flow, then it's time to think about physical assets like property. Once you have this in place, paper assets come next. Your mother and I have discussed property investment in great detail over the years. She probably knows more about it than I do!" Coach joked, "and she has done very well with it, so she can be a great resource for you in that department as well."

"What do you mean by paper assets, Coach?" Mitch asked.

"Paper assets are things like stocks and shares," he replied. "But let me give you the next paper to add to the book that Amy is going to write for me one of these days."

"Take a good look at what I've written," Coach said, leaning back in his chair. He wanted them to digest the difference between three types of assets.

> Business – property – stocks: when investing there are
> **ONLY THREE**
> real investments that meet the rule of having both capital growth and cash flow. I need to learn them in order of ability to make money from each. Business first: low liquidity, and high ability to add value, property second; medium ability to add value. Stocks last: high liquidity and low ability to add value.

"Note the order in which I have written them down. That is incredibly important, because that is the order in which I recommend you approach the capital ladder."

Coach continued to speak. "Business is your cash engine. It's the thing that generates the cash that you will need to invest in property and stocks. It also happens to have the highest ability to add value. This means that you can generate more cash flow simply by building the business. But it has low liquidity, which means it is difficult to turn the business into cash quickly should you need to. You would do this by selling it entirely, or at least selling a share of it to an investor, for instance."

Mitch was not interested in selling his sporting goods shop. He had worked so hard to build it, and he still felt passionate about it. After his years of diligent work, he had somewhat of an emotional tie to it. And besides, with his new BIG reason, a sporting goods store was the perfect asset to keep.

"So is that why you have placed property second, Coach?" Amy asked, "It isn't so easy to sell an investment property quickly if you needed to, and it also isn't easy to add value to it because it is usually subject to market value considerations." Amy learned this firsthand when she helped her mother years ago with her own property investments.

"That's right, Amy. So looking at stocks then, it would now appear obvious that they are easy to dispose of if you needed to, but you would have to be satisfied with what the market was willing to pay you for them. Hence, I have labeled them low when it comes to your ability to add value to them."

This made such good sense to Amy. She and Mitch had both dabbled in the market, and over the years these investments had pretty much evened themselves out.

"OK Coach, so let's assume I have great cash flow now, and I want to invest. Can you give us a quick rule of thumb as to how we would generally go about this?" she asked. She wasn't quite sure what she was hoping to hear, but she had a general feeling that there would be some kind of procedure or path that successful investors had found over the years. Again—no need to reinvent the wheel, as Coach always said.

"Let me see if I am reading you correctly. You are not after information about *how* to go about investing from here forward, or even what kinds of things to invest in, but what *type* of general categories you should be looking to, and in what order, so that you can not only learn as you grow but also make some more money on the journey. Would this be correct?"

"Yes, Coach, that's what I believe we are after. For instance, I have a feeling that it would be unwise to start a business from scratch. If I don't possess any business ownership experience, I would most probably make heaps of mistakes unnecessarily," Amy said.

Mitch agreed wholeheartedly. "Let me tell you, sis, I've made plenty. But now I feel confident in the way Nancy and I have systematized the store."

"That's quite right, both of you. There is a smart way of going about this, and there is the normal way most people do it. So let's start with another handout, shall we?"

Coach opened his file and selected a sheet.

"Now Mitch, you made an exception to this rule. You had a special opportunity, and I wanted you to take advantage of it, so I gave you my advice for that years ago. But usually, this is how the deals go." Coach allowed his students to read and digest the handout before speaking.

> Buy retail
> my first investments will involve buying into a **RETAIL DEAL,** and because of my lack of both knowledge and monetary capital, I will generally be **PAYING FULL** retail for my deals.

"What do you think this means, Amy?" he asked.

She thought for a moment before attempting to answer. "I suppose it means that when I get into business for myself for the first time, I should be paying full price, because I probably won't know any other way." Coach could tell she wasn't at all sure about her answer.

"Don't think of it as *should*, Amy. Think of it as *probably would*. You see, most first-time investors, be they business owners or people investing in the share market, will probably have no option but to get involved through some type of retail deal. In most cases, they simply won't have the ability or knowledge to become involved any other way. They will have no option but to pay full price."

Amy knew all about Mitch's special deal with Paddy and understood that these deals happened, but they were much rarer than the ones Coach just explained.

"Now don't get me wrong - this isn't always a bad thing. You have to get going somehow, you know. And you have to begin what I call your 'entrepreneurial apprenticeship.' This is where the learning process truly begins."

"But Coach," Amy asked, "surely there are other options available. I mean, with all the knowledge and experience available to us in this day and age, I must be able to go into business, and Mitch can expand his while avoiding all the basic pitfalls?"

"You're very perceptive, Amy. That's what I was going to mention next. In fact, it is the topic of my next handout." He opened his folder and took out the pages as he spoke.

Coach asked the twins to look at business as an investment option first. As Amy had earlier alluded to, he explained, there is a very good way to get into business without making all the usual mistakes most new business owners make: buy a franchise. It is a tried and tested business system that works. All the new business owner needs to do is adhere to the system, and the results will naturally follow.

> Retail business here I will be buying a franchise or similar, so **I WON'T HAVE** to learn everything at once. It's a great start. I get a system and support to **HELP ME** along my way to profits.

"But the thing with franchises is that they come at a cost," Coach explained. "Generally you need to pay the retail price for them, because this is how the franchise owner earns his money. This is the reward he or she gets for all the hard work they put in to developing and testing the system."

"So the downside with this is that you have to pay retail for the business, Coach, but the upside is that you generally hit the ground running?" Amy asked.

"Correct. And as you can see, there's nothing wrong with paying retail, is there? Bear in mind that it is within a well-systemized business that you will learn much about running a business. This is usually a great way to start."

Amy decided then and there she would seek a franchise for her next investment. She had the capital to buy retail, and it sounded like she could find something that would run itself relatively easily. In fact, she decided to start by purchasing a McConnell's Sporting Goods herself.

The three recapped briefly about property investments, but Mitch, Amy, and Kim all had experience with that—and Kim's only *real* session with Coach had been all about property investment. Mitch was the only one who wasn't quite up to par on property.

"Let's just review the definition of 'market value,'" Coach said. "It is the market price because that is what the market is prepared to pay, right? That is how we know that the true market value of anything is—it is simply the price that the market will bear."

"Okay, let's accept that as a definition of what market value means, Coach, but is there any other 'value' a property could sell for, then?" Mitch asked.

Coach smiled; this was something that had perplexed many property investors before him.

"Sure there is, Mitch, but we still need to look at shares. So let's consider them, shall we?"

The twins sat at full attention.

"I guess, just like property, we would start out buying shares at the retail price," Mitch continued. Coach nodded and opened his folder.

Retail shares mutual funds and other deals like just buying shares through **MY BROKER** are deals where I am paying full price and holding for a potential gain. **BETTER** than doung nothing, but still I am paying for my learning or lack of knowledge.

"Here again you will probably start off in the share market by buying retail. In most cases it simply can't be helped, as you will in all likelihood not be considered a *sophisticated* investor."

Mitch looked puzzled, but that was because Coach was obviously not inviting questions at this point. He decided to let it pass, though he suspected Coach would get to explaining things further at the appropriate time, as always.

"Once again, it's usually better to begin the process of investment than doing nothing, so don't consider the fact that you will be paying the retail price as something to stop you. You really do need to start learning somewhere."

"I guess this is one of the downsides to shares in general, Coach," Amy interjected. "I realize that the vast majority of share investors will never be able to avoid paying the retail price for their shares. What options do they have?"

"Good question, Amy. They really don't have any. That's one of the reasons why I place business and property ahead of shares on my list of preferred avenues to wealth creation. You have more control of the variables in them, whereas sophisticated traders take the choice pickings on the share market, and ordinary traders get to choose from the leftovers."

Mitch knew that Amy was well versed in matters like this, with her academic and business qualifications, so he didn't want to appear too naïve be asking silly questions. He was quite content to listen at this point.

"So if what we have been discussing is retail, what other way is there to buy?" Coach asked. Mitch took this as his cue to enter the debate.

"It would be wholesale, wouldn't it?" he replied. Coach nodded, as he gave them another handout.

"When you get to the stage where you have sufficient knowledge and money, your investing tends to take an interesting turn - you won't have to pay the retail price for anything anymore," Coach explained. "And it won't be because you will be 'in the know,' so-to-speak, but rather because you will have the contacts to help in this regard."

Buy wholesale - eventually I have enough

MONEY

and knowledge to start doing wholesale deals where

I CAN SKIP

giving the salesperson or company a sales commission.

"What do you mean by 'contacts' Coach?" Mitch asked. "That sounds almost underhanded, if you don't mind my saying."

"No, it's nothing like that, Mitch. Think of it this way: if you were a real estate agent, business broker or stock broker, who would you want to keep close as far as making sales is concerned?"

Mitch thought for a minute. He could tell that Amy was dying to answer.

"I'd keep in regular contact with the clients of mine who I knew had money and were looking for a quick sale; you know, the ones who wouldn't want to mess around trying to get a better price."

Coach signaled his agreement and pleasure that Mitch had understood the concept so easily. It saved him from having to explain it in greater detail.

"That's right, Mitch. So when you get to the point of becoming known by your local agents, they will get in touch with you very quickly when they come across a good deal. After all, it will be the easiest day's work for them if you were to snatch up their offering, wouldn't it? They would still get their commission, but this time it's just knowing who to contact to secure the sale. So for them, it's also about knowledge, isn't it?"

"I see exactly what you mean, Coach," he replied, pleased with himself. He knew his sister would also be impressed.

"So let's take a closer look at the three categories as far as buying wholesale is concerned, shall we?" he asked. The twins nodded. Coach handed them the next in his series of handouts and waited for them to finish reading.

> Wholesale business now I follow the **FORMULA** of buy, build and sell. I am buying well below market and using creative financing to get a great deal up front as well as making money on the back end. It **WAS WORTH** the knowledge and time investment to get to this stage.

"I love the idea of creative financing, Coach," Amy said, not knowing what to expect. "Isn't that kind of what Mitch did with Paddy and the sporting goods store? I must admit, it does sound a little dodgy."

Coach looked at her in surprise.

"Don't worry Amy, it's nothing of that sort, I can assure you. What I am talking about here is the type of finance deal that is not the norm in the retail sphere. Let me outline an example of this point."

She picked up her pen, opened her notebook, and prepared to take notes.

"Of course there's always the option of vendor financing to get a deal done. This is where the seller finances you to buy the business - they would accept repayments generated by the business. I have done deals where I pay for the business out of the monthly profits the business makes."

"Why would anyone want to sell a business that way?" Amy asked.

"Simply because it may be the only way they can sell the business," Coach replied, "And of course, the way Mitch bought the business from Paddy was very creative financing indeed."

"Okay," Coach continued on, "let's discuss wholesale property deals now, shall we?" Amy nodded. This was one area that interested her. She wasn't fully convinced that she would ever venture into business for herself, as she had more than enough to retire and live comfortably. Besides, she wanted to start on her ocean conservation and aquarium projects.

Coach handed each of the twins another sheet.

"As an investor, what determines the amount of money you make on an investment property when the time comes to sell it?" Coach asked. Mitch almost answered, then stopped himself. He suspected there was more to this than met the eye.

> Wholesale property now I am buying much better I know what I am doing, and **I'M MAKING** good money up front on my deals. I am generally following the buy, renovate, redraw system to make my money and **BUILD** my asset base.

"Give it a try, Mitch. What do you think?" Coach prompted.

"Well, I guess it all depends on how much you sold the property for, Coach. I mean, it stands to reason that if you sell for more, you make more."

Coach smiled and shook his head.

"No, that's not it, Mitch. But don't feel bad; that's the answer most people give. The amount you make is determined by the buying price, not the selling price."

"Say that again, Coach?" Mitch interjected, the surprise on his face clearly visible. He shot a quick glance over to his sister and was relieved to see that she, too, looked surprised.

"Think of it this way," Coach continued. "If you buy a property, let's say for $200,000, and you sell for $250,000, then you make $50,000. Now as we discussed before, the selling price would be market value, wouldn't it?"

The twins nodded.

"But what if you bought that same place for $180,000 instead of $200,000? How much would you make then?"

"$70,000 Coach," Amy replied.

"That's right. Because you are now an investor and are buying for the profit you will eventually make, you'll be trying to maximize this, won't you?"

Again the twins nodded in agreement.

"And who is really in control of the buying process? The buyer, or the seller?" Coach quizzed.

"Clearly the buyer," Amy replied.

"Why is it the buyer?" Mitch asked.

"Because the buyer is the one with the cash," Coach responded. "The buyer is the one who calls the shots. The buyer is the one who dictates the whole process. Just think back to when you sold your last home. Did you feel in control, or did you feel like the buyer held all the trump cards? I'm sure you found that it was the buyer, because if they didn't like or agree with what you were proposing, they would walk away and find something else. And if you consider the number of properties on the market at any one time, I'm sure you'll agree that it's hard enough to catch their attention and to get them interested, let alone to finally get them to submit an offer to purchase."

Amy knew all too well, from working with her mother on such deals, the logic of what Coach was saying.

"The agent's job is to get to the buyer on an emotional level, because then logic goes out the window and they lose the initiative. Your job as an investor is to buy only on logic and to avoid the emotion."

Mitch liked it when Coach gave those little nuggets of wisdom that would stick with him in every deal he did. This was one of them - it made so much sense.

"So how do we buy properties wholesale, Coach?" he asked.

"I first want to ask you what wholesale means."

"It means you are not paying the retail price, obviously," Mitch replied. "I guess it comes down to paying a price that doesn't take into account the middlemen." He looked at Amy for reassurance.

"I think it also applies to manufacturers selling goods to retailers," Amy added. "They are also wholesalers."

"That's right, but how does this apply to you as property investors?" Coach probed. "It's not as if you can avoid the middlemen here, is it? Chances are, you will still deal through the real estate agent."

Mitch looked puzzled. He scratched his head, deep in thought. Then he looked at Amy for clues. She had none.

"Think back to what we discussed earlier about market value," Coach prompted. "How does the market value affect your bidding for a property when you end up in a situation where you are not the only one interested in the property?"

"Ah, I see what you are getting at, Coach," Amy said. "So if we can get into a position where we don't have to compete for the property, we get to call the shots. We get the wholesale price," Amy concluded.

"That's it, Amy. So how can you get into a situation like that?"

"Well, mom and I went through a ton of real estate agents when I was helping her at first. It took a while to get to know a real estate agent well, one we trusted," she answered with a chuckle.

"You're not too far off the mark, Amy. We need to go back to the agent who knows that you are serious, have money, and are not going to waste time. They would be presenting your offer on the basis that it is for a quick sale, and if the seller refuses and wants to take their chances hoping for a higher offer, that higher offer may never come, and you may have bought elsewhere. So the pressure is on them to accept or not. What you achieve here is not having to compete with retail buyers who are buying on emotion. You are, in effect, a wholesale buyer."

Amy wrote as quickly as she could while Coach talked. It suddenly made so much sense. She wished she had known this when she was helping her mother, but she assumed that Coach had discussed this with her already, given that she had been very successful in investment properties.

"Can we do the same with shares, Coach?" she asked, as she finished the last sentence.

"Yes and no. You see, the situation is slightly different with the stock market. But first, here's another handout."

"Think back to when you first started trading shares," Coach began. "How did you go about it?"

Wholesale shares I am now ranked a **SOPHISTICATED** or professional investor and can get into deals that I never could before. I am also **FAR MORE** knowledgeable about derivatives and other great deals.

"We bought a small parcel of shares in a company that we liked, Coach," Amy replied. "I can't remember the exact circumstances, but it probably would have been in a company someone recommended to us at the time. Or it could have been one that was in the news."

"So what sort of prices did you pay?"

"Full retail, no doubt about it," Mitch chimed in. "But because we had to go through a broker—and I still don't see how we could do it otherwise—we probably paid way too much."

"And did you make or lose on the deal when you eventually sold?"

"I think we made. I can remember being really excited at the time," Amy said, looking to Mitch for concurrence.

"So then you may not have paid too much." Coach was prompting them to think.

"But if my profit is determined by my buying price and not the selling price, maybe we still got a raw deal, Coach." Mitch wasn't sure where this was heading.

"How much more could you have made on selling those shares if you had bought them for a lot less than you did?"

"A lot more, I give you that. But how could I have bought for less than the asking price?"

"You could have if you were a sophisticated investor, Mitch."

"So what exactly is a *sophisticated investor*, Coach? Isn't it just someone who is sharper than most?"

Coach chuckled a little. "No. A sophisticated investor is one who has a lot of money under management. The amount may vary from country to country, but generally you need to have somewhere around $1,000,000 to be considered a sophisticated investor."

Mitch raised his eyebrows in surprise. "How does having a lot of money help you to buy shares at a wholesale price?"

"It does by allowing you to buy before they hit the trading floor. You see, there are many instances when sophisticated investors get the jump on the general market. For instance, take companies that want to raise more cash through a stock offer. They instruct their underwriters or brokers to first offer shares to sophisticated investors or existing shareholders. One of the advantages of buying this way is that you may not have to pay brokerage fees. Second, the shares are usually discounted, so if you were to sell them as soon as they were listed for sale to the public, you would make an immediate profit."

"So it's another case of the rich getting richer, Coach," Mitch said with half a smile.

"It's how the economy is structured, Mitch. It needs entrepreneurs and investors, and as such, it tends to favor them."

It was Amy now who had something on her mind.

"Can you explain what derivatives are, Coach? I have heard about them and remember studying them when I got my MBA, but I never quite got around to finding out more about them."

"Sure, Amy. It is a financial product that gets its worth from the value of another product, hence its name. They include things like options, warrants, and futures. They are used by investors to either earn additional income from their existing shares or to protect their value."

Amy seemed relieved. She finished writing, closed her notebook, and leaned back in her chair. "Tomorrow I am going to see how I can use derivatives for myself. I'm going to call my broker and discuss my options, because I am concerned that a cooling economy is going to expose me to additional risk."

"That's great, Amy. This is what this learning experience is all about." Coach smiled, though he seemed a bit tired. They hadn't seen each other in years, and although they had asked for a visit "for a little advice," he knew it would turn into a full-blown session, and this had been a long one. He really felt like seeing it through with the twins, though. He would rather witness their ultimate success than to just cut bait and say he was retired. In fact, they were like family to him, so he would resume the sessions one final time.

Fortunately, Mitch yawned. It had been a long session for everyone, and he knew it wasn't over yet. Amy shot him a quick glance that made him feel like a little boy again. She still gave him "the look," just as she did all those years ago when they were in high school.

Coach saw Mitch's yawn as a sign that it was time to end the session for now. He asked them to commit to going over what they had learned this time, and to plan to do something positive with it. He led them through a quick planning session that involved deciding where they wanted to be in a month's time, and then taking actions to get there.

Amy wanted to investigate venture capitalists for her ocean conservation and aquarium. Mitch said that he was going to take a closer look at property and commit to setting up structures, so that he could benefit from buying wholesale. He also wanted to continue franchising his own sporting goods business while working out a plan to start a philanthropic effort to aid children who wanted to be involved in sports. Unfortunately, he couldn't afford it, and he didn't have the right support in place to participate.

Coach asked them to write down and sign their plans, like a contract. He counter-signed and reminded them that he was going to hold them accountable for the plans they had just put in place.

They set a date for Mitch and Amy to return in one month.

* * *

Once again, the twins drove to what they nicknamed the "Carlsbad Coaching Compound." As always, Gary the butler met them at the door, and Coach appeared shortly thereafter.

He started with a quick review of what they had undertaken to accomplish during the period since the last session. He then asked them to provide him with an overview of what had transpired. He listened intently as the twins spoke one at a time. They were both clearly excited at what they had achieved. Everything had gone according to plan.

Amy had set up a new account with her broker. Not only had she done additional research into the wonderful world of derivatives, she had attended a short course that her broker had recommended. She then issued instructions that enabled her to enter the market as a trader of derivatives. She also talked to several venture capital groups interested in environmental conservation, and was well on her way to raising funds to build a $40 million aquarium. That would not only support her conservation efforts with the money raised from ticket sales, but as Chairman of the Board, she would receive a decent salary to add to her already magnificent portfolio.

Next, Mitch outlined what he had done. He had formed a strategic alliance with a real estate agent in an area where he was interested in investing. The agent had agreed to contact him as soon as they had listed a property that met his investment criteria. He had spent a whole morning with the office principal, who had driven him around the area showing him the high and low points as far as attracting tenants were concerned. He then explained how much he was willing to spend and what return he was looking for from his investment. He told the agent that he had an insatiable appetite for investment properties, and would act quickly should the right ones turn up. Two days later he bought his first property, much to the agent's delight. He had established his credentials and received two more calls a few days later. These initially amounted to nothing, but the following day one of them offered a great deal, and he bought his second investment property for a fantastic price.

CREATE CAPITAL
eventually, I will have learned enough to start to put deals together for others to be a part of, and always keeping a percentage
FOR MYSELF.
The work to learn business, property, and investing was well worth it at this level of the ladder.

Coach was well-pleased.

"Massive action always leads to massive results," he reminded them.

"The topic I want to touch on today is that of capital," Coach said. He was mindful of not giving his students too much information at once. I was time for another handout.

"So now that you have cash flow from various strategies, it's time to create capital. How do you go about this, you might ask? Through putting deals together: deals that now involve other people. The beauty of this is that, through their involvement, you get to keep a percentage of what the deal is worth."

"What's in it for them, Coach?" Amy asked. She hadn't yet started to take notes.

"They get to leverage your knowledge, Amy. Remember, by now you know a lot about creating wealth; you have been learning this since you were 16. How many years is that?"

"My goodness, that's 24 years!" she replied in disbelief. "It really doesn't seem that long at all."

Mitch looked just as surprised.

"I guess when you put it that way, we probably do know a lot more than most people, Coach. I think they should be eager to tap into some of our knowledge and experience, for a price."

"That's exactly right. So don't be shy and undersell yourself. Concentrate on creating capital now; it's where you can continue to make significant progress on your path to wealth."

"So Coach, what avenues should we consider? I mean, what types of deals produce capital?"

CREATE business capital now my deals involve others investing their capital in my deals, and rather than buying companies, I am **SELLING** them, either through licensing or franchising.

"Good question, Mitch. Let me start by handing out another sheet."

"Let's start with business, because that is the place to start in most aspects of wealth creation, I believe. Remember what I said previously about being asset rich and cash poor?"

The twins nodded. This was one lesson Coach had stressed strongly: develop cash flow through business, and then invest that in assets like more business, property, or shares.

"One of the best ways of creating capital through your business is to get others to invest in your business, either through licensing or franchising your business. The reason this is so lucrative is because you only have to do the work of building your business and systemizing it once. Then, you sell it forever. This is a great way to create business capital, and Mitch, that was something you also had committed to looking into on your contract."

Mitch looked up and admitted he hadn't done all he could to learn about franchising. His franchises were doing well, but he may have jumped the gun by not learning more before beginning his franchise. "I understand that, Coach, but can you explain the difference between licensing your business and franchising it? I mean, why would you choose that route to raise business capital over the other?"

"Another good question. Let me see..." Coach leaned back in his chair and thought for a moment. He didn't want to get too technical, yet he needed to explain the different reasons as to why one approach may be preferable than the other in such a way that his students would understand how they could use either, should the opportunity arise.

"Most people would rather hit the ground running when entering the world of business ownership, especially for the first time. Many agree that it is pointless and a huge waste of money to make the same mistakes others have made before them if it is possible to avoid them. But to do so comes at a price. Successful business owners have systemized and documented exactly what to do to set up a business just like theirs. This is the basis of the franchise system. Do exactly what the system says, and you'll minimize your chances of failing or wasting money."

Amy furiously took notes, as she knew this is what Mitch really wanted to do with his business. He was finally beginning to see the potential here for his business and didn't want to miss anything.

"Franchising is not for everyone. Some business owners don't like the idea of following instructions to the letter. After all, this is one of the attractions of running your own business—doing it your way. But they still want the advantages of starting out with a successful product, business, or image. So they choose to either buy a licensed business, start one that is licensed to trade, or sell a well-known successful product or service. This way they have the advantage of the branding of the product or service they are selling, but they get to run the business the way they choose. See the difference?"

Mitch nodded. It was suddenly making sense how he could begin to create business capital. But it would have to be via the franchise route, because he didn't want his business concept watered down. Over the years, he realized the benefits of routine because this had been his main stumbling block as a youngster. He wanted to make sure that this didn't happen to others, especially considering that they were most likely seasoned athletes like him.

Coach could see that Mitch's mind had drifted, and he needed to bring him back to the present without dampening his enthusiasm. "Anything you want to share with us, Mitch?" he asked.

"I've just had a blinding flash of the obvious, Coach," he responded excitedly. "My shop is well-established now, and all my customers love it because it has been built around the concept of a football team. Players and casual sports fans alike hang out there all the time. They love the vibe of the place. They like that I always have the coolest new products before anyone else. It would be really simple to replicate it all over the country! Why hadn't I thought of it before?"

Coach was very proud. He knew his real function was to act as a catalyst for his clients.

"That's terrific, Mitch. Now what I want you to do when you get back to the office is start planning how you are going to go about franchising your business. What will you need to do first? How will you produce the systems? How much will you charge? All these questions need to be thought through. Will you have a plan ready for our next session?"

"You bet. It's already in my head - I just need to get it on paper."

"Good. So Amy, how are you going to raise capital for your operation?" Coach wanted to bring her into the discussion now.

"Well, seeing as how I can't create business capital for myself, I guess it will have to be through property investment and venture capital."

"Property is another excellent way to create capital. But before we begin out discussion on that topic, here's another handout.

> Create property capital
> I am now not just buying, but
> **DEVELOPING**
> and selling property, doing bigger deals.
> **THE TIME**
> I spent learning is well worth it.

"Once you have the ability to buy, renovate, and sell investment properties for yourself, what's stopping you doing the same, but this time with other people involved? What's the difference between a property deal worth $300,000 and one worth $3,000,000?"

Amy looked Coach straight in the eye, not sure how to respond.

"Apart from the obvious, I'm not quite sure what you are getting at, Coach," she replied sheepishly. Even though she knew Coach well enough to say what she thought and felt, questions like these still confused her.

"The difference is nothing but an extra zero, Amy. That's all."

Mitch looked surprised. "But that extra zero makes all the difference, Coach," he added. "And what a difference it is."

"Is it really that much, Mitch?" Coach challenged. "If you really think about it, the zero operates on two levels. In one way, it is not much different, because the amount of time and effort that usually goes into buying and selling a $300,000 house is about the same as a $3,000,000 house. But in another way, it makes all the difference! This is because what you stand to earn from the more expensive property is vastly greater than that from the less expensive property. Give it some thought for a moment, and you'll see what I mean."

Coach left them for a few minutes as he stepped out of the parlor. When he returned, the twins had had a chance to discuss the implications of what he had just said between them. They had reached a new level of understanding, and both of them felt fulfilled.

"So how did you two do?" Coach asked, as he made himself comfortable in his chair.

"Really well, Coach," Amy replied. "It's amazing how our existing beliefs can be so limiting. We've decided that we need to think big from now on. We see the benefits of doing so, and we also understand how leverage once again comes to the forefront."

"How do you think you can benefit from this?" Coach asked. "How can you capitalize on what you know?"

Amy thought for a moment before she replied. "I guess that there must be many investors out there somewhere who have the money to sink into the property market, but they lack either the time to find great deals or the knowledge about how to make it all happen."

"Or maybe both," Mitch added.

"That's right," Coach responded. "So how can you tap into this?"

"I guess there must be some way to make contact with them, Coach," she answered. "But I'm not sure I know how."

"Here's your homework for today then. Do a search on the Internet for property investor groups in your area. Contact your local real estate agent and ask if there are any such people that they know of. You need to get the word out that you are looking to make contact with other investors. Visit open houses on the weekend. Look for investor seminars. Talk to your bank manager. Think laterally here, and you will be surprised what happens."

Amy took notes as Coach spoke. She knew she was onto a winner here. She could feel it in her gut. Coach had told her many years ago that the surest sign that she was about to make a correct decision was when she felt either a fluttering in her stomach, or such excitement that she could hardly contain herself. Now was one of those occasions.

Create shares capital my

COMPANIES

are now of a size and ability to take to an IPO: it was really worth understanding the share market from

BOTH ENDS.

Coach still wanted to touch on one more topic before the session was through.

He opened his folder and selected the relevant page, where he slid two scrolls from the worn manila folder and handed them to Mitch and Amy.

"There's one more aspect to creating capital, and that is share capital," he said, as the twins glanced at the sheet.

Even before Amy had completed reading, Mitch looked over to Coach and asked: "What's an IPO, Coach?"

"Ah, I was wondering if you'd ask that. Most of my students do because it's not a well-known acronym."

He paused momentarily so Amy could join in the discussion.

"It's an initial public offering. I'm sure now you'll know what I'm talking about, don't you, Amy?"

"Yes, it's when a company floats on the stock exchange. I've bought quite a few shares that way over the years, and made quite a bit too, I might add," Amy replied, pleased with herself.

"So what's the purpose of an IPO, Mitch?" Coach asked.

"I guess it's to raise capital for an expansion or something similar," he replied.

"That's right. But remember, from the company's perspective it does bring with it certain compliance and reporting obligations. The real benefit of buying shares in cases like this is that the shares are usually underpriced when launched, and they usually rise quickly in price when traded on the open market, making those who got in on the ground floor potential fortunes."

Mitch looked over to his sister, who nodded. They had both done extremely well some years previously when their local electricity company went public. They sold their stocks within a week and realized a tidy profit. The shares stabilized soon after, and investors hadn't seen profits like that since.

"So how can you benefit from an IPO other than by buying shares in companies who have gone down this route?" Coach asked. "How can you benefit from both ends?"

"Would it be to take my business down that route, Coach?" Mitch asked.

"That's right, Mitch. That's something that you may want to think about for the future. It could bring in a lot of money for you and the company, but it will mean that you basically lose control of it as well. You will find yourself reporting to a board of directors and the shareholders. You will also find that your role will change, with the focus shifting firmly to ensuring that everything is done to prop up the share price."

The session had been extremely beneficial, and the twins had learned a lot. They also left feeling highly motivated and eager to do whatever it took to reach the next level in their individual quests for wealth. They had much to do when they arrived home, and they knew there was little time to waste.

They had come a long way since commencing their journey, but there was still much to achieve. Mitch had a feeling that somehow, this would be a journey without end.

Chapter 13

Reinvestment

It was a week after the twins' 45th birthday party. They had chosen to get together with their extended family to reflect on their lives so far. A board meeting of sorts, they said.

It wasn't difficult to see that they had come a long way - that was abundantly clear. They were what many would classify as rich, and they were comfortable with that. One of the things they had learned years prior was to understand what money was and how it could benefit them, their families, and their community.

Amy had never married. She loved the single life, as it afforded her all the freedom she could want to pursue her individual dreams and desires.

Mitch found his true happiness through his family. It was interesting to see how two twins could have such different values regarding the meaning of a perfect life. He now spent the vast majority of his time at home with his wife and teenage children. He liked it that way - it was a lifestyle choice that he was more than comfortable with.

They had done extremely well since their initial foray into property. Mitch had become something of a specialist in multiple dwellings, while Amy concentrated more on high-end homes and apartments. More than anything, she really enjoyed traveling the seas and diving while also working on her charitable environmental conservation organization.

McConnell's Sporting Goods now enjoyed the status of being a household name. They quickly sprung up in suburbs all over the country. Franchising had been the key to financial independence he had been looking for. Plus, he reveled in his role as chairman. He certainly had the charisma that sports-loving business people admired.

Success had become part of the twins' lives and those of their friends and family. Their positive "can-do" attitude had become their hallmark. Their friends didn't find it strange at all that young Kylie and Josh had shown an instinctive interest in following in their father's footsteps. They sat for hours and listened to his stories about Coach and how he had started out in life. They loved his football stories just as much as his business ones. And they loved it too when Auntie Amy came around and told them what it was like climbing the corporate ladder and building an aquarium for the community.

As the years went by and Josh and Kylie grew into young adults, Mitch and Amy found themselves informally coaching them as they themselves had been coached so many years prior. The tables had turned. The time had come to give back.

The time had also come to visit Coach one more time.

• • •

Two weeks later, Amy and Mitch settled down in Coach's parlor. Even though they no longer visited as regularly as they did years ago, they still enjoyed Coach's enthusiasm and energy. They viewed him now more as a friend and confidant than a mentor.

Amy had been talking a lot about living the lifestyle she spent the better part of her teen and adult years creating. She sensed the time was right to start thinking about settling down and being content with what she had achieved so far.

Mitch listened with interest, but wasn't so sure. After all, he was heavily involved in his franchise, and while this was consuming more and more of his time, he didn't mind; in fact, he loved it. He also started a successful charity for underprivileged children wanting to participate in sports, just as he had intended.

Amy had seen a potential "dream home" on the coast in Monterey, California. Being oceanfront property and just feet away from her "second world" thrilled her. She had first considered buying it as a positive cash flow property to add to her portfolio, but by her second inspection she began thinking that it would suit her as a residence. "Yes," she thought, "it is definitely time for a change." She liked the idea of consulting in the area of oceanic environmental conservation. Her expertise in this area had already earned her a great reputation, and she was finding herself in demand. Furthermore, it was something she really enjoyed doing.

She dreamily imagined sipping her coffee in the morning, watching the fog roll away, as she pondered her life. The fog would reveal more and more of the ocean's vastness, and she sat quietly to watch the sunset give way into indigo sky.

"So now we come to our final session," Coach said as he handed them each a sheet of paper. "I feel something like a bird does when the time eventually comes to see her babies take their final flight from the nest."

Amy could tell that the coach was choked-up with emotion.

"You both have been fantastic students and a pleasure to teach. I am really privileged to count you now as friends rather than students. And I am delighted that you have both taken absolute responsibility for your lives and done whatever you needed to do to achieve the goals you set for yourselves. The results are clear for everyone to see."

Amy didn't trust herself to answer; she looked over to her brother for support. She noticed tears in his eyes.

"What I have for you today is a brief discussion about what you should think about from here on out. You see, now that you have *made it*, it's not the end of the road. You still have certain responsibilities that come with the territory."

Spending my capital growth is **CRAZY.** Too many people sell their first investment property and go buy a boat. I must **REINVEST** my capital.

Coach picked up his copy of the handout and read it extraordinary quickly - a technique he had learned many years ago to help him overcome emotional moments.

"The first lesson today is to make sure you understand that you are not to spend all your capital growth. To do so is like killing the goose that lays the golden egg. Look after the proceeds of your effort. Nurture it, and it will reward you forever."

"That's something I learned the hard way, Coach," Mitch said. "I squandered my first few property deals, and I suppose the same can be said for the first few years I was in business. I lived it up based on the profit my shop made instead of reinvesting in the business. In hindsight, I now wish I had franchised the business years before I actually did."

"At least you have learned the lesson, Mitch. Most people never do. Another thing that most people who come into money don't realize is that along with it comes responsibility."

Mitch shot a quick glance at Coach, not quite certain that he had heard correctly.

Responsibility comes with wealth as I am now wealthy, or even rich, **I HAVE** a responsibility to teach others how to do the same, and to only teach those with the passion, desire, and integrity to use it **WISELY.**

"They have a responsibility, which is why they tend to lose it not long after they get it. Look at how many who win the lottery are still rich a year or two later—not many!"

He opened his folder and selected the penultimate handout.

Amy read the sheet and smiled. This was something

that had been on her mind for some time now. She knew Mitch felt the same, as he had recently begun teaching his children what he knew.

"You have probably realized by now that money attracts money. This is no idle cliché; it's a truism that has to do with the law of attraction. Likes attract, and opposites repel. Only those who truly deserve to have money will retain it for the long-term. You have to be a responsible custodian of it while it is in your possession, and you need to ensure that you pass on to others what you know about it. You need to teach those who will also use it wisely everything you know. Just as I have passed on this knowledge to you, you need to ensure that this knowledge is passed on to others, so that they can use it wisely for the greater good of all."

"Now is the time to give back," Coach continued. "It's part of your responsibility. See, not everyone will have the good fortune of being a custodian of a lot of money and knowledge. Support them, because while you were learning and making mistakes, they supported you. Both of you are giving back in significant ways, and one of the things you must pay forward is to teach others what I have taught you."

They chatted for another half hour like old friends. Their relationship had been extremely beneficial and profitable for all concerned. They had gained much from it: friendships, knowledge, fun, properties, business, and wealth.

Support the society that supported

ME.

The community that supported me is now mine to support with my time, skills, connections, and

MONEY.

"I want to leave you with just one more pearl of wisdom," Coach concluded. "If you look back over the past 29 years, the only real differences between you two then and now has been a result of the people you've met, the books you've read, and the actions you've taken. This is truly what it is all about. Go now, and encourage others to do the same; it is as much their responsibility as it is yours."

As they left Coach's office for the last time, Amy turned to Coach and said, "You know, Coach, I feel as though we have really achieved great things for ourselves. Just this morning I was thinking about our original BIG reasons for wanting to be wealthy. I am now a major contributor in the quest to preserve our oceans' beauty and share it with others. That includes a $40 million aquarium. I have established my own charity, and I also am the chairperson of a major conservation and research fund.

By contrast, Mitch changed his BIG reason along the way because their mom didn't need to be taken care of. So instead, he chose to take care of underprivileged children by coaching them, donating gear, and giving scholarships to child athletes who can't afford fees.

"Mom is giving back by training young women in what you have trained us, so that they will always be independent and able to care for themselves," Mitch stated with pride.

Coach smiled, nodding in agreement. He bade them farewell, knowing that he, too, had achieved his goal.